Common Embarrassing Mistakes in English
and How to Correct Them

by

Ann-Marie Lindstrom

United Research Publishers

Published by United Research Publishers

Printed and bound in the United States of America

ISBN 1-887053-12-3

Library of Congress Catalog Card Number 98-61611

Book design by The Final Draft, Encinitas, CA
Cover design by The Art Department, Encinitas, CA

Order additional copies from:

United Research Publishers
P.O. Box 232344
Encinitas, CA 92023-2344

Full 90-day money back guarantee if not satisfied.

Contents

Acknowledgments

This, like most books, was a collaborative effort. I get to put my name on it because I did most of the work, but I couldn't have done it without the assistance and encouragement of Karen Beck, Heather Dobbs and Richard Harrison. Mills is a relentless proofreader/editor: a most frustrating and valuable trait. Finally, thanks to Roger for giving me this opportunity.

Introduction

Some critics say English is a language dying from abuse and neglect. Newspaper and magazine articles have grammatical errors. Television reporters mispronounce and misuse words. Employers complain about job applicants who cannot spell. Supervisors have to teach employees how to write simple reports.

You should give yourself a pat on the back for becoming part of the solution to the problem by reading this book. I doubt you will want to sit down and read it front to back. While I have tried to make it clear and easy to read, it is heavy on the facts with little drama.

I hope you will find this book useful enough to keep on your desk and refer to from time to time. Not only will you help yourself by learning how to use the language better, you may become another language lover. When it is used correctly, it is rich and powerful.

Common Mistakes in English

How to Use this Book

It would be nice if I could say, "Read this book, and you will never write another poor sentence." Doesn't work that way. Unless you have a photographic memory, you can't remember all the rules and hints in this book. Professional writers and editors don't expect to remember everything. That's why we have so many books about English on our shelves.

Don't plan to read this book and then give it to a friend.

One way to use the book is to go to an area you know you have a problem with and then refer to other sections when you come across a concept you don't completely understand.

For example, if you start with adverbs, you may need to look at adjectives so you are sure of the difference. Or you may need to refresh your knowledge of sentence structure, if you have forgotten what a predicate is.

Even if you read the book from back to front, you would run into concepts before you get to the section where they are explained. I refer to clauses when

I describe and explain parts of speech, but must refer to parts of speech when I explain clauses.

☹ is a symbol we'll use to point out examples of bad things.

Make notes in the margins. Use a marker to accent areas you think you'll want to look at again. Add your own commonly misspelled and confused words, if I didn't include them.

Because I cover so many topics, you get the highlights. If you want to know more about a particular subject, check the bibliography for a list of books that go into greater detail. If the explanation and examples of a topic aren't clear to you, try checking another book. Every writer says things a little differently. Someone else's explanation may click for you.

Above all, don't get discouraged. No one was born knowing how to speak and write correctly. The more you write, the better you will get.

Parts of Speech

Every word in our language can be described as one or more of the eight parts of speech. Some words fit into more than one category, depending on how they are used. While it is highly unlikely anyone outside a classroom will ever ask you what part of speech a word is, it is difficult to use language correctly if you can't tell the difference between an adjective and an adverb. You can't follow the game if you don't know the players.

The eight parts of speech are nouns, pronouns, verbs, adjectives, adverbs, conjunctions, prepositions and interjections. This chapter will define each of them, give you examples and show how they are used.

Nouns

Nouns are generally people, places and things. *Astronaut, doctor, child, dinosaur, kitchen, desert, television, car* and *soccer* are nouns. A thing doesn't have to be something you can see or touch. *Air, truth* and the *United States of America* are also nouns.

Proper nouns

There is a special case of nouns that uses upper-case (capital) letters. They are called proper nouns. United States of America is an example. Others include Dr. Jones, Abraham Lincoln, Barney, Sahara Desert, Ford Escort and Sony. You can think of a proper noun as the name of a specific person, place or thing.

Sometimes you need to think about how you are using the noun to figure out if it is proper or not. If you are writing about dry, sandy places, you would use *desert*. If you are referring to a vacation destination, you would use Mohave *Desert*.

Collective nouns

A collective noun is a word for a group of individuals. Some collective nouns are

> *committee*
> *jury*
> *office staff*

When you speak of the group as a whole, the collective noun is singular so you use a singular verb.

> *The **jury has** an hour for lunch.*

Lunch hour applies to the whole jury as a group.

The collective noun is plural when you speak of

the individuals who make up the group. Use a plural verb in that case.

> The **jury have** *different opinions about his innocence.*

We are talking about the people who make up the jury. One body couldn't have different opinions.

Nouns are probably the easiest part of speech to understand. If you want to master them, work at using specific nouns when you can. A specific noun is stronger than a general noun with a string of adjectives in front of it. "My nephew is a rascal" is considered a better sentence than "My sister's son is a naughty boy."

Pronouns

Pronouns replace nouns. Writing and speaking would be very awkward without pronouns. Imagine saying

> *Johnny, Mother wants Johnny to walk the dog. Take the dog to Johnny's friend's house and throw the dog's ball for the dog to chase.*

How much easier to say

> *Johnny, **I** want **you** to walk the dog. Take **him** to **your** friend's house and throw **his** ball for him to chase.*

But wait a minute. Do you want Johnny's friend to chase a ball? And whose ball is it?

Following the rules for pronouns will make your sentences clear and easy to understand.

Types of pronouns

There are seven kinds of pronouns: personal, relative, reflexive, intensive, demonstrative, interrogative and indefinite. We will look at each kind.

Personal pronouns

Personal pronouns stand for a person or group of people. You decide which one to use based on whether the noun is singular or plural, how the noun is used regarding case and person, and the gender of the noun. The relationship between the noun and pronoun is called agreement.

Noun-pronoun agreement

Deciding if the noun is singular of plural is only tricky with collective nouns, but we told you about that in the noun section.

You already know a lot about pronoun case, even if you don't recognize that phrase. Pronouns have three cases: nominative, objective and possessive.

If the noun is the subject of a sentence or clause, you use the nominative case pronoun.

I called Tiffany on the phone.

If the noun is an object in the sentence, use the objective case.

*Tiffany called **me** on the phone.*

Use the possessive case to show ownership.

*Tiffany called **my** sister.*

When we talk about pronouns, person means something more than a human being. There are first person, second person and third person pronouns.

First person refers to the person speaking.

I am talking to you about her.

Second person refers to the person spoken to.

*I am talking to **you** about her.*

Third person refers to the person or thing being spoken about.

*I am talking to you about **her.***

Gender only matters in the third person singular. Usually the gender of a noun is obvious because people and animals are either male (masculine) or female (feminine). English generally uses the neuter *it* and *its* for singular objects; but ships are often referred to as *she,* and people may refer to objects like their cars as *he* or *she.*

Personal Pronouns

	Nominative	Objective	Possessive
		Singular	
1st Person	I	me	my, mine
2nd Person	you	you	your, yours
3rd Person, m	he	him	his
3rd Person, f	she	her	her, hers
3rd Person, n	it	it	its
		Plural	
1st Person	we	us	our, ours
2nd Person	you	you	your, yours
3rd Person	they	them	their, theirs

Here are some examples of how to figure out which pronoun to use:

*Mary got the promotion **she** deserves.*

Mary is one person, the subject of the sentence, the person talked about and female. We use the singular, nominative, third person, feminine pronoun *she.*

I** was so pleased to hear about **it.

I am one person, the subject of the sentence and

the person talking. We use the singular, nominative, first person pronoun *I*.

It substitutes for *the promotion*. The promotion is one thing, an object in the sentence and the thing being talked about. We use the singular, objective, third person, neuter pronoun *it*.

Possessive pronouns

Possessive pronouns show possession.

*The evaluation **her** boss wrote must have been a good one.*

Her substitutes for Mary and shows possession (in the grammatical sense, the boss belongs to Mary). We use the singular, possessive, third person, feminine pronoun *her*.

Some possessives stand alone, others go with a noun.

*The hard work was all **hers**, though. The promotion came from **her** dedication.*

The pronoun *hers* refers to Mary's hard work. In the second sentence the pronoun *her* stands only for Mary because the noun *dedication* is stated.

Except for *mine*, all the possessive pronouns that stand alone end in *s*.

Possessive pronouns are also used with gerunds— verb forms that end in -ing (more about them when we get to verbs). If you remember the gerund is used as a noun, it makes sense to use possessive pronouns with them. Most people don't use them, but you will be correct if you do.

Her *working hard finally paid off for her.*

Interrogative pronouns

Interrogative pronouns appear in questions. They do not refer to a noun or pronoun in the sentence.

The common interrogative pronouns are
  what
  who, whom, whose
  which

Here are some examples:
  Who *told you that?*
  Which *would you like?*
  What *did he mean by that?*

Relative pronouns

Relative pronouns refer to nouns or pronouns that occur earlier in the sentence. They introduce relative clauses that say something more about noun or pronoun referred to. The common relative pronouns are

that	*whom*
which	*whose*
who	

Here are some examples:

> The person **who** called at seven o'clock this
> morning doesn't know me well.
>
> I work swing shift, **which** was not my idea,
> and I was still in bed.
>
> It was weird, because the phone in the
> kitchen is the only one **that** rang.

Did you notice the clause beginning with *which* is set off by commas, while the other two examples weren't? That clause is nonrestrictive: some extra information that isn't vital to the meaning of the sentence. Always use *which* and commas with a nonrestrictive clause.

Reflexive and intensive pronouns

Those -*self* pronouns are called reflexive and intensive. They have exactly the same form, but slightly different uses.

As reflexives, they refer to the pronoun or noun acting as the subject of the sentence.

> **I** did it **myself.**
>
> The **cat** bit **herself** when she chased her
> tail.

As intensives, they emphasize another pronoun in the sentence.

> **I myself** did it.

They should only be used when referring to another pronoun in the sentence. You have probably seen them used incorrectly.

 Please return a signed copy to myself.

Demonstrative pronouns

A demonstrative pronoun points out something. There are only four demonstrative pronouns, and they are easy to understand.

The noun they stand for does not have to be in the same sentence. They have no case: use the same form for subjects and objects.

that: singular object at a distance
   Get that over there.

these: plural objects near the speaker
   I'll take these to the boss.

this: singular object near the speaker
   Do you want this report lying on my desk?

those: plural objects at a distance
   You can get those from shipping.

When these four words are used with nouns, instead of taking the place of nouns, they are called demonstrative adjectives.

The only difference between demonstrative pronouns and demonstrative adjectives is whether *that, these, this* and *those* stand alone (pronoun) or are used with a noun (adjective).

Interrogative pronouns

Interrogative pronouns ask questions. There are three interrogative pronouns; only one has different cases. The nouns they stand for are usually not in the same sentence.

The pronouns use the same form for singular and plural, so you have to think about the sense of the sentence to know whether to use a singular or plural verb. If the *what, which* or *who* you are talking about is singular, use a singular verb.

The interrogative pronouns and what they ask are
what: specific information
   What is going on here?

which: usually a choice
   Which plan are we going to use?

who: identity of a person
   Who is in charge?

Who is the only one with different cases:
who in the nominative case
   Who has the report?

whom in the objective case
   To whom should I forward the report?

whose in the possessive case

Whose copy of the report is lying here?

Indefinite pronouns

Indefinite pronouns refer to nonspecific nouns. Use these when you don't know who, what or how many of something you are referring to. Because they are so flexible, you should be careful not to overuse them. Too many indefinite pronouns make your writing weak.

Here is a list of indefinite pronouns, which use the same form for the nominative and objective cases:

all	*most*
another	*neither*
anybody	*nobody*
anyone	*none*
anything	*no one*
both	*nothing*
each	*one*
either	*other*
everybody	*some*
everyone	*somebody*
everything	*someone*
few	*something*

Many indefinite pronouns have the same form in the singular and plural. You need to think about what the pronoun stands for when choosing the verb form to use. Look at these examples:

Most of the dishes were cleared off the table.
We are talking about more than one plate, so we use a plural form (*were*) of the verb.

Most of the table was cleared.
We are talking about an area of one table, so we use a singular form (*was*) of the verb.

Verbs

Verbs show action or state of being. They say what the nouns *do* or *are.*

Verbs that *do:*
run
  I run every morning.

believe
  Do you believe that?

sell
  Can I sell you a bridge, too?

Verbs that *are:*
am
  I am not an athlete.

feel
  I feel healthy, though.

Notice the previous sentence talks about *how* I feel, not *what* I feel. When we talk about what I feel, the word is an action verb.

> *I feel the weight of my past sins—burgers and fries for lunch.*

The difference between *action* and *state of being* verbs is important when you start looking at what follows the verb.

Linking verbs

Linking verbs are the ones that show a state of being. There is no action you can see. Linking verbs do not take an object, but they are followed by a complement. A complement says something about the subject of the sentence.

A complement that renames the subject is called a predicate noun.

> *My dog is a **Jack Russell terrier**.*

Jack Russell terrier is another name for *my dog*.

A complement that modifies the subject is called a predicate adjective.

> *He is very **energetic**.*

Energetic modifies *he*. It tells you something more about him, rather just giving you another name for him.

The most common linking verb is *to be*. Some other linking verbs are:

appear

> *Dinner appears to be almost ready.*

become

> *I've become very hungry.*

feel

> *I feel weak with hunger.*

grown

> *The children have grown restless.*

look

> *My father looks like a hungry man.*

remain

> *In spite of all the activity, my mother remains calm.*

seem

> *She seems happy.*

smell

> *The pumpkin pie smells delicious.*

sound

> *The kitchen sounds busy.*

taste

> *The turkey tastes wonderful.*

Auxiliary verbs

Auxiliary verbs are used to create other verb forms. Some auxiliary verbs are also verbs by themselves, but others only work with other verbs. Use an auxiliary verb to form past tense or passive voice.

My dog has gone to obedience school three times. [active]

He has been kicked out of obedience school three times. [passive]

Notice how each of the common auxiliary verbs below change the meaning of the sentence *I invite my neighbors to a party.*

be (*am, are* and *is* are forms of the verb)

I am inviting my neighbors to a party.

have

I have invited my neighbors to a party.

will

I will invite my neighbors to a party.

should

I should invite my neighbors to a party.

would

I would invite my neighbors to a party.

may

I may invite my neighbors to a party.

can

I can invite my neighbors to a party.

might

I might invite my neighbors to a party.

could

I could invite my neighbors to a party.

must

I must invite my neighbors to a party.

ought

I ought to invite my neighbors to a party.

do

I do invite my neighbors to a party.

Transitive and intransitive verbs

Verbs can be transitive or intransitive. A transitive verb takes an object. The action carries (*trans,* as in transport) across to something.

I fired my assistant yesterday.

My assistant is the object of the verb *fired.* I did the firing and my assistant is who was fired.

An intransitive verb doesn't need an object.

She didn't work very hard.

Didn't work is the verb and it doesn't have an object. The verb doesn't act on anything. It stands alone.

On the other hand, if my assistant didn't work the cash register correctly, the verb *didn't work* would have an object—the cash register.

Principal parts of verbs

Verbs have different forms depending on how they are used. You build the different forms from the principal parts. The three principle parts are called present infinitive, past tense and past participle.

We are going to look at these forms and use the technical names for them, but don't let the names throw you. When you look at the examples, you'll see that you already know a lot about verbs in general.

First we'll define the principle parts and then give examples of the exceptions (irregular verbs). In the next section, we'll talk about how they are used.

Present infinitive

The present infinitive is the technical word for the basic form of a verb. The past tense and the past participle are built from the present infinitive.

Past tense

Form the past tense of regular verbs by adding *-d* or *-ed* to the present infinitive. Add *-d* to words that end in *e; -ed* to those that don't.

Past participle

With regular verbs, the past participle is formed the same as the past tense—add *-d* or *-ed* to the present infinitive.

Irregular verbs

Well, that was too easy. Here comes the catch. Irregular verbs don't follow any rules at all. You may notice some of them look similar to each other, but there is no way to predict which will be similar. You have to memorize them, or at least recognize them so you can look up the principle parts.

A dictionary will show you the past tense and past participle of an irregular verb. If you don't see anything but the present infinitive, you can assume the verb is regular and add *-d* or *-ed.*

This is a list of the most common irregular verbs:

pres. infinitive	past tense	past participle
bear	bore	borne (carried)
		born (given birth)
beat	beat	beaten
begin	began	begun
bend	bent	bent

pres. infinitive	past tense	past participle
bid	bade	bid (at an auction)
bid	bade	bidden (request)
bite	bit	bitten, bit
bleed	bled	bled
blow	blew	blown
break	broke	broken
bring	brought	brought
burst	burst	burst
catch	caught	caught
choose	chose	chosen
come	came	come
dig	dug	dug
dive	dived, dove	dived
do	did	done
draw	drew	drawn
drink	drank	drunk
eat	ate	eaten
fall	fell	fallen
fight	fought	fought
flee	fled	fled
fly	flew	flown
forget	forgot	forgotten
freeze	froze	frozen
get	got	got, gotten
give	gave	given
go	went	gone

pres. infinitive	past tense	past participle
grow	grew	grown
hang	hung	hung (objects)
hang	hanged	hung (people)
know	knew	known
lay	laid	laid
lead	led	led
lend	lent	lent
lie	lay	lain (as in *rest)*
lie	lied	lied (untruth)
lose	lost	lost
pay	paid	paid
read	read	read
ride	rode	ridden
ring	rang	rung
rise	rose	risen
run	ran	run
see	saw	seen
set	set	set
shake	shook	shaken
shine	shone	shone
sing	sang, sung	sung
sink	sank, sunk	sunk
sit	sat	sat
slide	slid	slid
speak	spoke	spoken
spend	spent	spent

pres. infinitive	past tense	past participle
spring	sprang	sprung
steal	stole	stolen
swear	swore	sworn
sweep	swept	swept
swim	swam	swum
swing	swung	swung
take	took	taken
tear	tore	torn
throw	threw	thrown
thrust	thrust	thrust
wear	wore	worn
weep	wept	wept
wring	wrung	wrung
write	wrote	written

Verb voice

Voice indicates whether the subject performs an action—active voice—or is acted upon—passive voice.

*Sue **brought** potato salad to the picnic.*
Sue (the subject of the sentence) performed an action.

*The potato salad **was brought** by Sue.*
The potato salad (the subject of this sentence) didn't do anything: it was acted upon.

You can change a sentence written in active voice

to one in passive voice by making the direct object the subject.

Only transitive verbs can take passive voice form, since they have direct objects but intransitive verbs don't.

Active voice is generally a better choice for your writing. It is stronger. Occasionally, the person or object acted upon is the important part of an idea, so you want it to be the subject of the sentence. Most of the time, though, passive voice is a sign of someone trying to sound formal and official.

The first sentence below is a better sentence than the second.

Supervisors will submit quarterly evaluations of their staff.

Quarterly evaluations of staff will be submitted by supervisors.

Verb mood

Mood indicates if the speaker thinks of a sentence as a fact, a command, or something in doubt or contrary to fact. The three moods in English are indicative, imperative and subjunctive.

Statements and questions are in the indicative mood. Commands are in the imperative mood. There is nothing special about them.

We talk about them only to introduce the subjunctive mood. The subjunctive mood expresses doubt, regret, wishes or something contrary to fact.

*If I **were** you, I wouldn't do that.*

This is a statement contrary to fact. I am not you. Notice *I were. Were* doesn't usually go with *I*. Only in the subjunctive mood.

*If he **were** a good manager, we'd all be in better shape.*

The subjunctive mood changes how you use the verb *to be* in the singular first and third person in the present and past tenses.

I wish I were taller.

I wish he were taller.

I wish she were taller.

I wish it were taller.

Another place you may encounter the subjunctive mood is in a formal meeting. You often hear:

*It is resolved the contract **be** awarded to Tiffany's Towing Company.*

*I request the city manager **give** a full report.*

The rule for the last sentence is that third person singular verbs drop their usual final -s.

The subjunctive is mainly used in formal situations these days, so be careful with it.

Verb tense

Tense indicates when the action of the verb happens. There are subtle differences among the 24 tenses (bet you didn't know there were that many). These differences can make your writing precise and strong. You don't need to remember what each tense is called, but do learn the differences.

Here are explanations of each tense with examples. Only twelve are listed, but each can be active or passive. That makes a total of 24.

present: what happens right now
 I swim at the YMCA.
Use the present infinitive of the verb.

past: what happened
 I swam at the YMCA yesterday.
Use the past tense of the verb.

future: what will happen
 I will swim at the YMCA tomorrow.
Use the present infinitive with the future form of the auxiliary verb *to be.*

present perfect: what began in the past and continues into the present
 I have swum at the YMCA for months.
Use the past participle with the present tense of the auxiliary verb *to have.*

past perfect: what began further in the past, before something else

> *I had swum at the YMCA for three months*
> *before they re-tiled the pool.*

Use the past participle with the past tense of the auxiliary verb *to have.*

future perfect: what has not happened yet, but will be completed in the future

> *I will have swum 1,000 miles by the end*
> *of the year.*

Use the past participle with *will have.*

present progressive: what is happening on a continuing basis, not only now

> *I am swimming every day.*

Use the present participle with the present tense of the auxiliary verb *to be.*

past progressive: what happened in the past on a continuing basis

> *I was swimming at the YMCA all summer.*

Use the present participle with the past tense of the auxiliary verb *to be.*

future progressive: what will be happening, on a continuing basis, in the future

> *I will be swimming at the YMCA next week.*

Use the present participle with *will be.*

present perfect progressive: what began in the past, continues into the present and will continue into the future

> *I have been swimming at the YMCA since April.*

Use the present participle with the present tense of the auxiliary verb *to have* and word *been.*

past perfect progressive: what began further in the past and continues in the past, before something else

> *I had been swimming for several weeks before I started feeling stronger.*

Use the present participle with the past tense of the auxiliary verb *to have* and the word *been.*

future perfect progressive: what will end at a particular time in the future

> *In a few months, I will have been swimming for year.*

Use the present participle with the compound auxiliary verb *will have been.*

The next page has a chart summarizing verb tenses.

	Simple Form	**Progressive Form**
		Active Voice
Present	I move	I am moving
Past	I moved	I was moving
Future	I will move	I will be moving
Present Perfect	I have moved	I have been moving
Past Perfect	I had moved	I had been moving
Future Perfect	I will have moved	I will have been moving
		Passive Voice
Present	I am moved	I am being moved
Past	I was moved	I was being moved
Future	I will be moved	I will be being moved
Present Perfect	I have been moved	I have been being moved
Past Perfect	I had been moved	I had been being moved
Future Perfect	I will have been moved	I will have been being moved

Adjectives

Adjectives modify nouns. Language would be dull without adjectives. Would you rather have a piece of cake or a huge piece of moist, chocolate cake?

Basically there are two ways adjectives modify nouns. They increase the noun's meaning by adding detail, or they separate the noun from other similar nouns.

Descriptive adjectives

Descriptive adjectives describe nouns (what a surprise, eh?). Think of them as adding detail, color, or your feelings and impressions.

> *The attractive woman wore a tiny, black dress to the party.*

Attractive describes the woman; *tiny* and *black* describe the dress.

Limiting adjectives

Limiting adjectives indicate a specific noun or quantity of nouns.

> *Three other women showed up in the same dress.*

Three limits how many women showed up; *same* indicates which dress we are referring to.

Here are the five kinds of limiting adjectives:

possessive	*my, your, our*
demonstrative	*this, that, those, these*
interrogative	*which, what, whose*
articles	*a, an, the*
numerical	*one, each, several*

Comparative and superlative forms

Another thing to remember about adjectives is descriptive adjectives come in three forms: positive, comparative and superlative.

Let's take a look at the adjective *funny* in its different forms. Positive adjectives make no comparison, they just describe.

*Phil is a **funny** guy.*

Comparative adjectives state one noun is or has more of something than another noun.

*Jack is **funnier** than his brother.*

Superlative adjectives declare a noun has the highest degree of something among a group of three or more nouns.

*Their mother is the **funniest** person I have ever met.*

The general rule for one-syllable adjectives is to add -er to the positive adjective to create the comparative and -est to make the superlative.

hard	*harder*	*hardest*
red	*redder*	*reddest*
old	*older*	*oldest*

Two-syllable adjectives may use the *-er* and *-est* convention, or they may have *more* and *most* in front of them.

pretty	*prettiest*	*prettier*
	more pretty	*most pretty*

Adjectives longer than two syllables should use *more* and *most*.

intelligent	*more intelligent*	*most intelligent*
athletic	*more athletic*	*most athletic*

Adjective position

It is important to pay attention to where you place an adjective in a sentence. Make sure it is close to the noun you mean to modify. If you get sloppy with an adjective, the sentence may not mean what you intended. Look at these sentences.

Only *I ruined my friend's birthday party.*
This means everyone else behaved themselves.

I ruined my **only** *friend's birthday party.*
This means I don't have many friends (and may not have any after the party!).

I ruined my friend's **only** *birthday party.*
My friend had never had a birthday party before.

Adjective form

You may be able to recognize some adjectives by their endings. Here are common endings of adjectives created from nouns or verbs.

-able	fashionable, unbelievable
-al	financial, magical
-ary	elementary, secondary
-en	wooden, rotten
-ful	thankful, beautiful
-ible	incredible, comprehensible
-ic	metric, historic
-ily	easily, bodily
-ish	amateurish, fiendish
-ive	massive, inventive
-less	friendless, homeless
-ous	humorous, enormous
-some	worrisome, loathsome
-y	stony, woody

Adverbs

Adverbs modify verbs, adjectives and other adverbs. They are trickier than adjectives because of their multiple uses, but you can master them.

Adverbs and verbs

When adverbs modify verbs, they usually say something about how, how much, where or when the action took place.

> *The kids behind us talked **loudly** all through the movie.*

Loudly describes how they *talked*.

> *I asked them if they could quiet down a **little**.*

Little says how much *quieting down* I wanted them to do.

> *One of them leaned **forward** and said something very rude to me.*

Forward tells where he *leaned*.

> *I am **seldom** shocked, but he stunned me.*

Seldom describes when I *am shocked*.

Adverbs and adjectives

A noun can be modified by more than one adjective or by an adjective modified by an adverb. This isn't as confusing as it sounds, though you may have to think a moment to decide which way to do it.

> *A **beautifully** dressed woman joined us.*

The adjective *dressed* modifies *woman*, and the adverb *beautifully* modifies *dressed*. The sentence doesn't say anything about the woman's attractiveness—just that her dress is beautiful. Notice there is no comma between the adverb and adjective.

A beautiful, dressed woman entered the room.

In this sentence the woman is both dressed and beautiful. *Beautiful* (an adjective) and *dressed* (an adjective) both modify *woman*. We don't know if she is wearing a gorgeous outfit or a flour sack. Use a comma between the two adjectives.

Adverbs and adverbs

Only another adverb can modify an adverb.

*The beautiful woman **seemingly unintentionally** attracted every man's attention.*

Conjunctive adverbs

Adverbs used as conjunctions are called conjunctive adverbs. They carry the thought from one independent clause to another.

*She was pleasant to everyone; **nevertheless**, every other woman in the room disliked her.*

Conjunctive adverbs use a semicolon and a comma in formal writing. Even when the conjunctive adverb appears in the middle of one clause, the clauses are joined with a semicolon.

*The beautiful woman talked to other women; they noticed, **however**, she kept looking at the men.*

Here are some common conjunctive adverbs:

besides
consequently
furthermore
hence
however
indeed
likewise
moreover
nevertheless
namely
still
then
therefore

Conjunctive adverbs are fairly sophisticated parts of speech. They add precision to your writing. That means you need to be careful with them.

When you use *consequently,* be sure the clause following it really is caused by the first clause.

Common adverbs

Many adverbs are formed by adding *-ly* to an adjective.

rude   *rudely*
careful *carefully*

Not all *-ly* words are adverbs, though. Some adjectives have that ending: *friendly* and *womanly,* for example. Also, there are the adjectives formed from nouns by adding *-ily.*

Some adverbs have the same form as their corresponding adjectives: *fast, much,* and *late* are just a few.

The only reliable test for an adverb is how it is used in the sentence. If the modifier is working on a verb, an adjective or another adverb—it is an adverb.

Common errors

The most common problem with adverbs is *not* using them. People, who are either careless or don't know any better, use adjectives to modify verbs or other adjectives.

> *The boy talked rude to me.*

Rude is modifying *talk,* which is a verb, so the modifier should be an adverb. The adverb form is *rudely,* not *rude.*

Don't use *when* and *where* instead of a noun. This is a misuse I bet you hear once a week, if not once a day. A book published in 1935 mentions this error. It still sounds uneducated today.

☹ *A trade show is **where** you meet potential customers.*

*A trade show is **a place to** meet potential customers.*

🙁 *Working overtime is **when** you make good money.*

*Working overtime **is a chance** to make good money.*

Conjunctions

Conjunctions join together words, phrases and clauses. There are three kinds of conjunctions: coordinating, subordinating and correlative.

Coordinating conjunctions

Coordinating conjunctions join words, phrases and clauses of equal importance.

Use them in a series of nouns or adjectives.

***Mary, Tom** and **Pete** were all considered for the job.*

*The job requires **intelligence, patience** and **thick skin.***

Use coordinating conjunctions to join together two or more phrases of equal importance.

*The new manager is responsible **for hiring** and **for firing.***

Use coordinating conjunctions to join together two independent clauses of equal importance.

Mary didn't get the job, and **she is happy.**

Notice the comma before the coordinating conjunction joining two independent clauses.

Subordinating conjunctions

Subordinating conjunctions join less important sentence parts to the more important part. How the phrase or clause is used in the sentence determines the punctuation.

The common subordinating conjunctions are:

after

I'll see you after the meeting.

although

I have to be there, although I think it is a waste of time.

as

I will leave as soon as I can.

because

I have to be there because I called the meeting.

before

I'll call you before I leave my office.

if

Let me know if you can get there by noon.

since

I've missed you since last night.

so that

I'll hurry so that we can have a leisurely lunch.

than

I'd rather have lunch than meet for dinner.

that

Let's go to the restaurant that is across from the bank.

though

I called the meeting though it made my boss mad.

unless

Unless he causes trouble, the meeting will be dull.

until

I'm counting the days until I leave this job.

when

Did I tell you the news when I talked to you last night?

whenever
> *Whenever I buy a lottery ticket, I start dreaming.*

where
> *I don't know where I am going to move.*

wherever
> *Wherever I go, I'll travel first class.*

while
> *Be quiet while I tell you how big the jackpot was.*

Correlating conjunctions

Correlating conjunctions are always used in pairs to join sentence parts of equal importance. Here are some common pairs with the parts joined together highlighted:

both...and
> *She was both **thrilled** and **nervous** to hear of his good luck.*

either...or
> *He was going to either **propose** or **say good-by**.*

neither...nor
> *She'd neither **expected** nor **hoped** things would happen this fast.*

not only...but also

*She was tired of him because he was not only **boring** but also **stupid.***

whether...or

*A man she could love had to be interesting, whether **rich** or **poor.***

When using correlative conjunctions, be sure the parts joined have the same structure. Don't join a clause and a phrase with a correlative conjunction.

☹ *She was tired of him not only **because he was boring** but also **stupid.***

See how *also* now connects just a single word, while *not only* connects the clause *because he was boring*. This is not a good sentence. The original sentence is better because both correlative conjunctions connect single words.

Prepositions

Prepositions show a relationship between words.

*Put the cat **in** the refrigerator.*

(shows relationship between cat and refrigerator)

Here are some of the most common prepositions.

at

Meet me at the merry-go-round.

between

I can't choose between taking a bath or mowing the lawn.

by

I drove by the beach last night.

for

He's wanted for murder, you know.

from

Derek ran away from his baby-sitter.

in

Put your hand in mine.

of

I need a bucket of green paint.

on

Sit on the couch, and stop pestering the dog.

through

He put his fist through the door.

to

We are going to Happy Hour after work.

with

I'll have a pizza with everything.

The biggest problem you will probably encounter with prepositions is deciding which pronoun to use with them. The pronouns are objects of the prepositions, so use the objective form. Those are *me, you, him, her, it, us, you* and *them.*

   Come **with me.**

People seem to have trouble when there is more than one pronoun.

   *Will John come **with him** and **me**?*

The hint is to say the sentence with only of the pronouns. You wouldn't say, "Will John come with I?" So don't be tempted to say, "Will John come with him and I?"

Here are some prepositions that can be tricky.

into: expresses motion from one place to another
   *The fireman ran back into the burning build-
   ing to rescue the child.*
in: designates a place
   The fire started in the kitchen.

between: speaking of two
   *I can't decide between marrying Jack or
   going to Paris.*
among: speaking of more than two
   She is the only blonde among all the girls.

on: designates a place
   The cat is on the dining room table again.
upon: expresses motion
   He leapt upon the stove yesterday.

The distinction between *on* and *upon* isn't used much these days.

beside: by the side of
  He sat down beside the beautiful redhead.
besides: in addition to
  After a short conversation, he realized she was smart besides being attractive.

by: introduces the agent
  I was hit by a flying brick.
Here the brick was acting on its own.

with: introduces the tool
  I was hit with a brick.
In this example, someone used the brick to hit me.

Interjections

An interjection is a funny little part of speech to express emotion. It doesn't have a grammatical connection to the rest of the sentence. It usually appears at the beginning of a sentence.

Some words are only interjections; they do not show up in any other form. A few of these are *oh, ouch* and *whew.*

  Oh, *this dinner was wonderful.*

Some words are another part of speech in addition to being an interjection.

Goodness, *the check is bigger than I expected.*

If the interjection shows mild emotion, set it off from the rest of the sentence with a comma. Stronger emotion calls for an exclamation point.

Wow! *Look at how much the wine cost.*

Common Mistakes in English

Sentence Structure

Sentences are the framework of our language. All the parts of speech need to fit together right for the framework to support our ideas. The purpose of language is communication. You want people to understand what you are trying to tell them. Because you have many different ideas and different reasons to share those ideas, you need to know how to put together words in various ways.

We will discuss the fine points of writing in a later chapter. First we need to establish the ground rules. That means understanding sentences.

Definition of a sentence

A sentence is a group of words that expresses a complete thought and usually has a subject and a predicate. The subject says what or who the sentence is about. The predicate says something about the subject and includes a verb.

You live is a complete sentence. *You* is the subject. The sentence is about you. *Live* is what you do; it is the predicate of the sentence. It may not be an exciting sentence, but it is a sentence.

We usually dress up our sentences a bit more.

You *live in the city.*

The subject is still *you.* The predicate has expanded to *live in the city.*

Let's expand the subject.

My cousin with the pierced lip and green hair lives in the city.

If I had written just *My cousin with the pierced lip and green hair* it would not be a sentence, even though it has many more words than the original two word sentence: *you live.*

It would not be a sentence because it has no predicate. There is no verb. This colorful cousin isn't doing anything.

I can make it a complete sentence with one minor change:

My cousin has the pierced lip and green hair.

Now the predicate is *has the pierced lip and green hair.* Adding the verb *has* made all the difference.

A sentence must have a predicate, but it can exist without a subject. Sometimes the subject is implied. Sentences without subjects are most often commands or requests. The person you are speaking to is the implied subject. *Wake up!* is an example.

Sentence parts

All the words in a sentence serve some function. As you read about sentence parts you will see references to parts of speech.

Written and spoken words are parts of speech and sentence parts at the same time.

You can think of the part of speech as the name for the word. The sentence part is like a job description for the word.

Subject

The subject of a sentence states who or what the sentence is about. The subject is one or more nouns or pronouns with their modifiers. Clauses or phrases that work as nouns can be the subject of a sentence.

> **We** *will work late all next week.*
> **The entire staff** *will work late all next week.*
> **Working late** *isn't fun.*

Verb

The word *verb* can mean a part of a sentence or a part of speech. When you are talking about the part of a sentence, it may be also called the simple predicate. We'll call it the verb.

The verb of a sentence describes an action or state of being connected with the subject. It tells you want the subject does or is. In the passive voice, it means what happened to the subject.

*We **will work** late all next week.*

*The staff **isn't** happy.*

*We **were told** it is necessary.*

Compound predicates

Sentences can have compound predicates. A sentence with a compound predicate has two verbs, but the subject is only written once.

*The staff is **unhappy** and **grumbling.***

That's pretty obvious. More complicated sentences with compound predicates are sometimes mistakenly seen as compound sentences.

*The staff is **unhappy** about having to work late and **grumbling** to anyone who wants to listen.*

Remember that compound sentences will have two subjects. The sentence above has only one subject: *the staff.*

Let's look at a couple more examples of compound sentences versus compound predicates. Notice how they have different meanings.

I went to the grocery store, and I took a bath. [two separate activities]

I went to the grocery store and took a bath.
[They probably won't let me come back!]
Paul and Victor were at the park, and we didn't see them. [We didn't see Paul and Victor.]
Paul and Victor were at the park and didn't see them. [Paul and Victor didn't see some other people.]

Recognizing the difference between compound sentences and compound predicates will move you into the ranks of skilled writers.

Direct object

The direct object receives the action of a verb. It answers the question what? or whom? after the verb. The direct object is one or more nouns or pronouns. Clauses or phrases acting as nouns can be the direct object. Direct objects use the objective case for pronouns.

*We got **a memo** today about working late.*
A *memo* is what we got.

*I wonder **how I can avoid it.***
How I can avoid it is what I wonder.

*My mother is visiting **me** next week.*
Me is whom my mother is visiting.

Indirect object

Indirect objects receive the direct object. The indirect object usually appears before the direct object. You can't have an indirect object unless you have a direct object. An indirect object is a noun or pronoun. Indirect objects use the objective case for pronouns.

*The boss sent **me** a memo today.*
The boss sent a memo [direct object] to me [indirect object].

*I gave **my assistant** a copy.*
I gave a copy [direct object] to my assistant [indirect object].

Predicate noun

A predicate noun follows a linking verb and renames the subject. The predicate noun can be a noun or pronoun. Clauses or phrases acting as nouns can be the predicate noun. Even though the rule is that predicate nouns should use the nominative case for pronouns, common usage accepts the objective case much of the time.

*I will be **a busy person** next week.*
A busy person [predicate noun] is another name for I [subject] in this sentence.

*Next week is going to be **a nightmare.***

Next week is the subject; nightmare is another name for next week.

*I am already **stressing.***
Stressing is a gerund phrase acting as a noun.

Predicate adjective

A predicate adjective follows a linking verb and describes the subject. The predicate adjective is an adjective. Notice the difference between a predicate adjective and predicate noun. The predicate adjective tells you something more about the subject with an adjective, while a predicate noun calls the subject by another name with a noun.

Let's take the predicate noun examples and replace the predicate nouns with predicate adjectives.

*I will be a **busy person*** [noun modified by an adjective] *next week.*
*I will be **busy*** [adjective] *next week.*

*Next week is going to be a **nightmare*** [noun].
*Next week is going to be **horrible*** [adjective].

*I am already **stressing*** [gerund acting as a noun].
*I already feel **stressed*** [adjective].

Stressed out is a participle phrase acting as an adjective. It describes how I feel. In this sentence, the linking verb *feel* shows a state of being.

You see the meaning of the sentences is practically identical. A logical question at this point is, "Why do we care what we call them, if predicate nouns and predicate adjectives can say the same thing?"

No one outside a classroom will ever ask you to describe the difference, but you will write better sentences if you know the difference.

Sentence type

Sentences can be classified four ways based on their meanings: declarative, interrogative, imperative and exclamatory.

A declarative sentence makes a statement or declares something.

Most of the sentences we use every day are declarative.

An interrogative sentence asks a question and uses a question mark. An interrogative sentence can start with an adverb like *why* or *where*, or an interrogative pronoun—*what, who* or *which*. Interrogative sentences without the *wh-* words almost always put the verb (at least part of it) before the subject.

Why don't people ask more questions?
Aren't they curious?

An imperative sentence makes a request or command. Often imperative sentences don't show the subject. *You* is the implied subject.

Answer my question, please.

An exclamatory sentence expresses strong emotion and uses an exclamation point. Exclamatory sentences should be used sparingly. They lose power if they are overused. You want them to stand out from the rest of your writing. Think of them as shouting. If you talk loudly all the time, people won't know something important is happening when you start shouting.

I asked you a question!

Sentence classification

Sentences are classified by their structure as simple, compound, complex and compound-complex. The classification depends on the clauses used to create the sentence. We discuss clauses later in this chapter.

Simple sentences have one independent clause.

This is a simple sentence.

Compound sentences have two or more independent clauses.

This is a compound sentence [independent clause], *and it could have been two sentences* [independent clause].

Complex sentences have one independent clause and one or more dependent clauses.

I could have written the last example as two separate sentences [independent clause], *if I'd wanted to* [dependent clause].

Compound-complex sentences have two or more independent clauses and one or more dependent clauses.

You will probably never be asked to identify a compound-complex sentence [independent clause], *after you leave school* [dependent clause], *but knowing about them will make you a better writer* [independent clause].

Clauses

Clauses have subjects and predicates just as sentences do. They can be dependent or independent. Dependent clauses are sometimes called subordinate clauses. You need to recognize whether a clause is dependent or independent before you can correctly punctuate sentences. It isn't too hard.

Independent Clauses

The only difference between an independent clause and a sentence is how it is used. An independent clause can stand on its own as a simple sentence. That's why it is called independent. It doesn't have to be alone, though. It can form compound sentences with other independent clauses. It can support dependent clauses in complex sentences.

Independent clauses are the workhorses of English. A nice, clean independent clause is a joy to read. It expresses one idea without much decoration.

Sometimes a little decoration is good. Sometimes you want variety in your writing. You can add dependent clauses to make sentences more interesting.

All the sentences in the independent clause section are simple sentences. Each one is an independent clause.

Dependent clauses

Even though both dependent and independent clauses have subjects and predicates, dependent clauses cannot stand on their own.

If you look at the last sentence, you'll see a dependent clause before the comma.

If someone said to you, "Even though both dependent and independent clauses have subjects and predicates," you would wait for her to continue.

You'd want to know *even though* what? Those first eleven words of that sentence are important, and they have meaning, but they cannot stand alone. They do not make an independent clause.

Here are some examples with the dependent clauses marked with a *D;* independent, an *I.*
> *When the sun goes down, [D] the fun begins [I].*
> *I often sleep through the entire morning [I] because I stay up late. [D]*
> *My brother, [part of the I] if I remember correctly, [D] likes to go to bed early. [the rest of the I]*

A dependent clause is either an adjective clause, adverb clause or noun clause depending on how it is used in the sentence.

Adjective clauses
Adjective clauses are used as adjectives.
> *My cousin **who has a degree in accounting** cannot find a job.*

The dependent clause *who has a degree in accounting* modifies *my cousin.* It says something about my cousin. It is working as an adjective.

Adjective clauses are generally introduced by relative pronouns. We talked more about relative pronouns in the chapter called Parts of Speech, but here is a list of the common ones:

that	*which*
what	*who*
when	*whom*
where	*whose*

Adverb clauses

Adverb clauses do the work of an adverb; that is, they modify a verb, an adjective or another adverb.

> *He hasn't been called for a second interview* **since he got his lip pierced***.*

Since he got his lip pierced modifies the verb *hasn't been called.* It gives you more information about when, where, why or how the action happened.

> *His mother thinks the green hair,* **though it is a lovely shade***, may have something to do with his difficulty.*

Here *though it is a lovely shade* says more about the adjective *green.*

*He stubbornly refuses, **which is out of character**, to acknowledge the connection.*

Which is out of character modifies the adverb *stubbornly* in this sentence.

Adverb clauses are introduced by subordinating conjunctions or relative pronouns. The common subordinating conjunctions are:

after	*though*
although	*unless*
as	*until*
because	*when*
before	*whenever*
if	*where*
since	*wherever*
so that	*which*
than	*whichever*
that	*while*

Noun clauses

Noun clauses are used as nouns in a sentence. If you replaced an entire noun clause with one word, the sentence would still make sense. It wouldn't mean quite the same thing (you use noun clauses to put more detail into the sentence than a single word would), but it would still make sense.

That he is a nonconformist *doesn't endear him to many employers.*

That he is a nonconformist is the subject of the sentence. We could substitute the noun (with its possessive pronoun) *his attitude* for that clause and the sentence would be basically the same.

That dependent clause is working as a noun. Noun clauses are usually built into the main clause just as a noun would be. Sometimes they are introduced by

that	*why*
whether	*when*
how	*where*

Many writers overuse *that* in their sentences. Remember a noun clause does not have to be introduced by *that*. Check your writing to see if you can take out a *that*. Authorities estimate 50% of the *that*s in most writing can be eliminated without harming the sentence meaning. In fact, the strongest writing has no extra words.

Phrases

Phrases do not have a subject and a predicate. Phrases are incomplete thoughts and should not be used alone.

Phrases can act as adjectives, adverbs or nouns. Let's look at the clauses examples again and see how they are different when we substitute phrases.

My cousin **who has a degree in account-ing** [clause] *cannot find a job.*
My cousin **with a degree in accounting** [phrase] *cannot find a job.*

The phrase *with a degree in accounting* does the same job of modifying *my cousin* as the clause *who has a degree in accounting*. Notice the phrase doesn't have a verb, while the clause did.

He hasn't been called for a second interview **since he got his lip pierced** [clause].
He hasn't been called for a second interview **since his lip piercing** [phrase].

Again a phrase, *since his lip piercing*, replaces a clause, *since he got his lip pierced*. This change may not be as obvious, because *since* can function as a conjunction and as a preposition.

In the clause *since* is a conjunction. In the phrase *since* serves as a preposition. The big clue is the verb. Phrases don't have verbs; clauses do.

His mother thinks the green hair, **though it is a lovely shade** [clause], *may have something to do with his difficulty.*
His mother thinks the green hair, **a lovely shade** [phrase], *may have something to do with his difficulty.*

The phrase *a lovely shade* modifies the adjective green, just as the phrase *though it is a lovely shade* does.

> He stubbornly refuses, **which is out of character** [clause], *to acknowledge the connection.*
>
> He stubbornly refuses, **acting out of character** [phrase], *to acknowledge the connection.*

The phrase *acting out of character* might look as though it has a verb—*acting*—but the word is working as a noun here. It is called a gerund and we'll talk about those a little later in the chapter. You'll just have to trust me for now.

> **That he is a nonconformist** [clause] *doesn't endear him to many employers.*
>
> **Being a nonconformist** [phrase] *doesn't endear him to many employers.*

Being a nonconformist is another phrase with a gerund—*being*. The phrase is the subject of the sentence, just as a noun would be and as the clause *that he is a nonconformist* was.

Now that we have shown how phrases function, we need to look at the forms they use to do the work.

Prepositional phrases

A prepositional phrase consists of a preposition and its object. Prepositional phrases can function as nouns, adjectives and adverbs.

Under the bed is very dusty.
Here we are talking about a place we call *under the bed*, so the phrase is acting as a noun.

*The doll **under the bed** is very dusty.*
In this sentence *under the bed* describes the doll, so the phrase is acting as an adjective.

*The dusty doll is lying **under the bed**.*
This time *under the bed* modifies the verb *lying*, so the phrase is acting as an adverb.

Verbal phrases

Another kind of phrase is a verbal phrase. Verbal phrases begin with participles, infinitives or gerunds and are followed by an object.

Participle phrases

Participle phrases act as adjectives, so they modify nouns or pronouns. They use either the present participle of a verb—*carrying*—or the past participle of a verb—*carried*.

*The girl **carrying luggage** is my daughter.*

Carrying luggage is acting as an adjective, modifying *the girl*. If there are four girls in the room, you know the one with the luggage is the one I mean.

When you see an *-ing* word, check for a linking verb (some version of the verb *to be*) in front of it. If the sentence includes something like *is carrying*, *carrying* is functioning as a verb.

My daughter **is carrying** [verb] *luggage.*
The *-ing* form without *to be* is the beginning of a participle phrase if it acts as an adjective.

The first sentence includes *is*, a version of *to be*, but it belongs to *the girl*, not to *carrying*.

The past participle of a verb is also used in participle phrases. Past participles usually end in *-ed*, *-t* or *-en*.

The luggage, **packed with most of her worldly possessions**, *is heavy.*
The participle phrase *packed with most of her worldly possessions* modifies luggage. It tells you additional information about the luggage.

Did you notice how one sentence set off the participle phrase with commas, and the other one didn't? In the sentence without commas, the phrase is built into the sentence. It is an important part of the sentence, because without that phrase you wouldn't know which girl I'm talking about.

In the sentence with commas, the participle phrase is a little something extra. The main message of the sentence is the luggage is heavy. You don't need to know what is in the luggage to understand it is heavy.

A participle phrase that begins a sentence will almost always use a comma before the main clause.

> **Struggling with those heavy suitcases**, she looks so young and small.

Infinitive phrases

Infinitive phrases act as adjectives, adverbs or nouns. They use the infinitive of a verb—the word *to* followed by the verb stem.

> She won't run out of clothes **to wear** anytime soon.

The infinitive phrase *to wear* acts as an adjective modifying the noun *clothes* in this sentence.

> She went **to buy** more socks last night.

Here the infinitive phrase is *to buy,* acting as an adverb to modify the verb *went*. The phrase says why she went.

> She loves **to shop**.

The infinitive phrase *to shop* is acting as a noun.

It is the object of the verb *loves.* It is a noun, because it is something she loves. If it doesn't look like a noun to you, think of other things she might love: candy, money, books and her mother. *To shop* is as much a noun as each of them.

You know these are infinitive phrases instead of prepositional phrases (which can also start with the word *to)* because phrases don't have objects.

Your English teacher may have told you not to split infinitives (put an adverb between *to* and the verb stem). That rule has become a minor concern. Split infinitives are increasingly acceptable in casual speech.

Here's an interesting tidbit about split infinitives: *The Oxford Companion to the English Language* says, "Probably the most famous split infinitive in the language is *to boldly go (where no man has gone before)* ... from *Star Trek."*

Gerund phrases

Gerund phrases always act as nouns. They use the *-ing* form of a verb without a linking verb.

> **Moving to New York** *has always been my daughter's dream.*

Moving to New York is the subject of this sentence.

Did you notice that participle phrases and gerund phrases both use the present participle? Bet you are wondering how you can know which is which. You need to look at how the phrase is used in the sentence. If the phrase is used as an adjective, it is a participle phrase. If it is acting as a noun, it is a gerund phrase.

> ***Moving to New York*** [noun; subject of the sentence] *has always been my daughter's dream.*
>
> *My daughter has always had a moving to New York* [adjective; modifying dream] *dream.*

One way to remember the types of verbal phrases is the acronym PIG: Participle, Infinitive, Gerund. It isn't a very elegant memory tool, but it is odd enough to stick in your mind.

Odds are no one will ever ask you to identify a participle phrase. You will just feel more confident about your sentence structure once you know they exist, what they look like and how they act.

The important thing is to recognize the differences among sentences, clauses and phrases.

Punctuation Marks

Apostrophe '

Apostrophes show possession or indicate missing letters in a contraction.

> *My grandmother's dog barks too much. I hate him at three o'clock in the morning.*

Apostrophe and possession

To show that something belongs to a noun or indefinite pronoun, you make the noun or pronoun possessive.

Please notice we are talking about indefinite pronouns, not possessive pronouns. You don't need to add an apostrophe or *s* to possessive pronouns. Use them in their original forms: mine, yours, his, hers, its, ours, theirs.

If the noun or indefinite pronoun (either singular or plural) does not end in *s*, simply add *'s* to form the possessive.

> *Gram's dog is too nervous.*
> *Children's yelling makes him bark like crazy.*

If the singular noun ends in s (no singular indefinite pronouns end in s), add 's, unless the extra s makes the word difficult to pronounce or changes the pronunciation.

The bass's fishy smell made the hungry dog bark.

This rule applies to proper names, too.

The barking woke up Mrs. Jones's baby.

Jesus, Moses and names that end with an -eez sound are traditional exceptions. You simply add an apostrophe after the final s with those names.

Jesus'
Moses'
Euripides'

When a plural ends in s, add the apostrophe after the s.

My other grandparents' dog is much calmer.

Related nouns are treated like a unit if they possess the same thing, and you add the 's only to the last noun.

I've never heard my aunt and uncle's dog bark.
Los Angeles and San Diego's freeways are too crowded.

Apostrophe and contractions

The other main use for apostrophes is to show missing letters in contractions. We use these all the time. Here are common ones:

he is	*he's*
is not	*isn't*
I will	*I'll*
could have	*could've*

The biggest confusion about apostrophes is probably *its* and *it's*. This one makes lots of people crazy: some can't bear to see it misused, while others can't figure out which to use.

It's is a contraction of *it is.*

Feed the poor dog. **It's** *hungry.*

Contractions use apostrophes. When you mean *it is*, write *it's*.

Its is a possessive pronoun.

Did you feed the dog **its** *dinner?*

In this sentence, *its* does not use an apostrophe. None of the possessive pronouns (*mine, yours, his, hers, its, ours, theirs*) use apostrophes.

While not quite a contraction, dates some times leave off the first two digits. An apostrophe replaces the missing two digits.

There was great music in the '60s.

Did you every wonder why we write *o'clock*? It stands for *of the clock.*

Apostrophe and plurals

Apostrophes are used with plurals in only a few cases.

To avoid confusion, letters used as nouns take apostrophes with plurals.

> *Vanna, show us all the* T's.
> *Mind your* p's *and* q's.

Plural abbreviations with periods take an apostrophe.

> *The room was full of Ph.D.'s and M.D.'s.*

Acronyms do not take apostrophes with plurals.

> *Both YMCAs in town will be closed today.*

Plural numbers, either written as words or numerals, do not take apostrophes.

> *Swing dancing is almost as popular as it was in the 1940s.*
> *I love watching the kids dance in twos and threes.*

People misuse the apostrophe often when they work with plurals. Certain plurals, proper names and numbers, seem to attract unnecessary apostrophes.

☹ *The Smith's are coming to dinner.*

1950's

Neither of those uses of the apostrophe is right.

Learn when to use the apostrophe with plurals, and you will be better than the average writer.

Asterisk *

You don't see asterisks much anymore. If you want an informal footnote, an asterisk works nicely. Stick it at the end of a word* and then put another asterisk at the bottom of the page with whatever extra you want to say about the word.

You can impress some people just by knowing what it is called. Please remember it is an as-te-risk, not an as-te-riks.

Slash (bar, diagonal, solidus or virgule) /

This handy little punctuation mark has a few totally unrelated uses. It has more names than uses! You might be able to win a bet if you remember solidus (pronounced *solid-ess*) and virgule (rhymes with *fur fuel*) are two of its names.

You can write dates with diagonals in informal use. The convention in the United States is to write month/day/year. One reason formal writing demands fully written dates is that in Britain dates are abbreviated as day/month/year.

November 25, 1987, can be written as 11/ 25/1987.

Fractions written with numerals use diagonals. If you have a whole number with the fraction, separate them with a hyphen. See the section on numerals for rules about writing numbers as words and numerals.

The baby weighs 11-1/2 pounds.

When you write a sentence that could use either one of two words and still make sense, you can indicate that by using both words and separating them with a diagonal.

All **permanent/temporary** *employees are covered by Workers' Compensation.*

The diagonal can also mean *per,* as in *miles/hour,* in either casual or technical writing.

The satin for her wedding dress cost $25/ yard.

The acid concentration is 15 ml/liter.

Brackets [ ]

Brackets are another vanishing punctuation mark. Their primary use is to insert editorial comments. When you encounter brackets, remember what's inside them is not part of the original material. Instead, it will be information an editor thought you ought to know. It may be an addition, a correction or a comment.

"The people of this great state [California] are proud to claim the American [National] League champions, the San Diego Padres."

California is in brackets to name the state. You might want to do this when the meaning would be unclear without the addition.

In this case, if the governor of California made this statement in a speech he could just say *this great state.* On the other hand, if a national magazine printed part of the speech, it might be a good idea to insert the name of the state.

The second set of brackets holds a correction to the original text. Obviously the writer was not a baseball fan, because the Padres play in the National, not the American, league.

The politician said, "The only reason I'm running for office is to serve the people. [Yeah, right.] And I promise to keep your interests in mind."

This set of brackets holds a comment made about, not by, the speaker.

On those rare occasions when you want to place a parenthetical expression inside parentheses, you can use brackets.

When the salesman called yesterday about the widget order (I've promised him delivery by Thursday [check with shipping on this]), we discussed the possible strike.

Capitalization

We will cover the basic guidelines for capitalizing words, but there are always exceptions. Legal writing, for example, has its own rules for capitalization. If you do any kind of specialized writing, you should check style guides for that field.

Capitalize the first word in a sentence.

The merry band of shipping clerks delivered our presents.

Capitalize the first word in a direct quotation (unless you start the quotation in the middle of a sentence).

Mr. Swanson told us, "We wish you all a happy holiday."
The rest of his speech was boring until he got to "bonus checks at the front desk."

Capitalize I, the first person singular pronoun.

Everyone's ears perked up at that, I think.

Capitalize people's names.

George Washington
Neil Thomas

Capitalize titles when they appear immediately before the person's name.

Everyone loved President George Washington.

Do not capitalize titles when they are separate from the name.

Everyone loved George Washington, our first president.

Capitalize continents, countries, states, counties and cities.

North America
United States of America
California
San Diego
Strafford County, but *county of Strafford*

Capitalize the street names, including Road, Street, Avenue and the rest.

Main Street
Cypress Boulevard

Capitalize the nicknames for places or areas.

Bay Area (San Francisco)
Dixie (the South)
Land of the Rising Sun (Japan)

the Loop (Chicago)
the Village (New York)

Capitalize the regions of the country.

New England
the East Coast
Mid-Atlantic states
Mid-West
the South
the Southwest
the Northwest

Though we capitalize the words east, south, west and north when we refer to parts of the country, do not capitalize them when they are used as directions.

Turn north at the intersection by the bank.
The compass is reading south by south-west.

Capitalize the names of lakes, rivers, oceans, mountains, islands and the like.

Lake Michigan
Mississippi River
Atlantic Ocean
Mount McKinley
the Hawaiian Islands

The generic term for the place—lake, river, ocean and the rest—is also capitalized if it appears at the beginning of more than one of the places.

Lakes Tahoe and Crater

Rivers Ohio and Missouri

Do not capitalize the generic term if it appears after the plural names.

the Ohio and Missouri rivers

Capitalize buildings and structures.

Statue of Liberty

White House

Golden Gate Bridge

Capitalize organizations and government offices.

American Red Cross

Boy Scouts of America

House of Representatives

Department of Labor

Court of Appeals

Capitalize schools, colleges, universities.

E.O. Green Junior High School

Grinnell College

Old Dominion University

Capitalize months and days of the week.

January

Tuesday

The seasons are not capitalized.

winter

spring
summer
autumn
fall

Capitalize historic events and holidays.
Civil War
Renaissance
Ground Hog Day
Fourth of July

Capitalize trademarked names. This is an important issue if you write for the public. If a trademarked name starts to appear with a lowercase first letter in documents, a company can lose the trademark protection. The ™ symbol is only necessary on packaging and in business documents.
Chrysler
Pepsi-Cola
Xerox

Some trademarked names have peculiar capitalization. Follow the pattern a company uses.
WordPerfect
CorelDraw

Use the following rule to capitalize titles of books, magazines, plays, movies, television shows and music:

Capitalize every word that isn't a conjunction,

preposition or article. Capitalize the first and last words even if they are articles, prepositions or conjunctions.

Bedtime for Bonzo

Of Thee I Sing

The Way of All Flesh

Journal of Irreproducible Results

Pictures at an Exhibition

Colon :

A colon signals to the reader that something is coming. It may be a long quotation or formal explanation.

Lincoln's best speech is the Gettysburg Address: "Four score and seven years ago ..."

Installing your new hard drive is simple: First unplug your computer ...

It may be a summary or expansion of what was stated before.

He likes fast cars, contact sports and action movies: all manly things.

He likes manly things: fast cars, contact sports and action movies.

Do not use a colon in sentences that introduce a series of things with a preposition.

He likes manly things like fast cars, contact sports and action movies.

Don't use a colon to separate a series of things from a verb.

The manly things he likes are fast cars, contact sports and action movies.

A colon is used at the end of the salutation in a business letter.

Dear Mr. Johnson:

Use a colon to separate hours from minutes when you write them as numbers.

10:36 p.m.

Bible chapters and verses are separated with a colon.

Genesis 9:5

Colon position

Place the colon outside both quotation marks and parentheses.

I read some of my favorite short story in freshman English: "The Lady or the Tiger," "The Necklace" and "The Lottery."

I can still remember the first line of my favorite poem, "The Wreck of the Hesperus": "It was the schooner Hesperus that sailed the wintery sea."

We lived all over the country (when I was a child): New Hampshire, Virginia, Illinois, Indiana and California.

Comma ,

The comma is the most frequently used punctuation mark. A sentence with one period at the end may have three or four commas. A comma can join, separate, enclose, introduce or indicate omitted words. Commas used correctly can make your writing clearer and decrease the chance of misunderstanding. That's the good news.

Mastering the comma might take some practice. Look at the examples for each rule.

Commas and independent clauses

Use a comma to separate independent clauses joined with coordinating conjunctions.

I stayed up too late last night, and I still got to work on time today.

Watch out for sentences with compound predicates rather than independent clauses.

I stayed up too late last night and still got to work on time today.

If both independent clauses are short and related, you may leave out the comma. This is a judgment call, because there is no definition of short. If either independent clause has more than five words, you are probably better off using the comma.

I sang and he danced.

I went to the movies with my sister, and he worked on his car.

Comma splice

Using the comma without a conjunction is called a comma splice. Don't do it!

☹ *I got involved in a mystery novel, I forgot to go to bed.*

Don't forget to the conjunction when you use a comma to create a compound sentence from two independent clauses.

I got involved in a mystery novel, and I forgot to go to bed.

Commas and introductory clauses and phrases

Use commas to separate introductory modifying clauses and phrases from a main clause. The key words are introductory and modifying.

Introductory means the clause or phrase appears at the beginning of the sentence. It introduces the main clause.

The clause or phrase might not take a comma if it came later in the sentence. Moving it to the front of the sentence from its natural place is the first clue that it may need a comma, but being introductory isn't enough. The clause or phrase must also modify a part of the main clause.

To be considered an accomplished writer,
you must use commas correctly.

The introductory phrase in the sentence above modifies the subject *you.*

Modifying means the clause or phrase adds extra information about the main clause. Just as adjectives and adverbs modify other parts of speech, clauses can modify other parts of sentences.

Sometimes the introductory clause or phrase is the subject of the sentence. Then it is acting as a noun. Don't use a comma then.

To be considered an accomplished writer
had always been his goal.

When the modifying introductory clause or phrase is short, you may omit the comma as long as the meaning stays clear without it.

After we talked I hung up the phone.

Watch for sentences that are unclear without a comma.

After hitting Paul ran the bases.

This sentence could use a comma.

After hitting, Paul ran the bases.

Commas in series

Use commas to separate words, phrases and clauses in a series. If you have three or more words, phrases or clauses written in a series, use commas and a conjunction.

The rule for comma use in a series has changed a few times in the past several decades. Right now most of the authorities say to use a comma after all but the last word, phrase or clause.

> *Please bring a blanket, some charcoal, and a beach chair to the picnic.*

You may notice this book doesn't use a comma before the conjunction. Most authorities want that last comma, but not all. I don't like the last comma, so I don't use it—unless not using it would cause confusion.

> *I used to listen to Barry Manilow, Neil Diamond, and the Captain & Tennille.*

If you choose not to use the last comma, be careful about times when it is necessary for clarity. Most importantly, be consistent. Don't use the last comma sometimes and leave it out other times.

If you use the unusual pattern of linking all the items in a series with conjunctions (for emphasis), don't use any commas.

> *We are all going to Gramma's tomorrow:*

your brother and your sister and your fa-
ther and you and I.

When you have a series of clauses that already
have commas in them, you should use semicolons
to separate. That way the separation between clauses
is clearer.

Six of us are going to the party together:
John and Mary, who live next door; Fred
and Suzie, who live across the street; and
my husband and I.

Commas and adjectives

Use commas to separate adjectives modifying the
same noun.

The old, gray mare ain't what she used to
be.

Old and *grey* both say something about the mare.

Watch out for adverbs modifying adjectives, though.
Don't use a comma to separate them.

Her costly [adverb] *designer* [adjective] *gown*
was ruined when she fell into the pool

Don't use a comma when one adjective has a stronger attachment to the noun than the other. A trick
is to see if you can reverse the adjectives and have
the sentence mean the same. If you can't, the adjectives are not separated by a comma.

We made wild grape jelly last summer.
Wild modifies *grape jelly,* not just *jelly.* You wouldn't talk about *grape wild jelly.*

Sometimes an adjective and noun are so closely related they become a unit. *Short story* is an example. Don't use a comma when you add another adjective to those combinations.

My aunt doesn't like modern short stories.

Commas and cities and states

Use commas to separate a city and state and to separate the state from the rest of the sentence.

My brother was born in Portsmouth, Virginia, at the Naval Hospital.

Commas and numerals

Use commas in numerals (numbers not written in words) over one thousand, except in four-digit dates and all addresses. Commas should separate the number into groups of three (1,000; 1,000,000).

There were more the 150,000 people at the parade.
In 1984, they found remains of a camp from 10,000 B.C.
The parade passed right by 1600 Pennsylvania Avenue.

Commas and dates

Use commas to separate a date from the rest of the sentence if the full date is given. Use a comma between the day and the year, and between the year and anything following.

The meeting was on October 15, 1995, in Cincinnati.

You don't need to use commas if only the month and year appear.

They went to Europe on vacation in August 1996.

Commas to contrast

Use a comma to separate contrasting parts of a sentence.

I asked him to come in today, not tomorrow.

You said you wanted Tom to help, not Jack.

Commas for clarity

Use a comma to separate parts of a sentence that might be misread.

During the winter of 1978, 300 people suffered frostbite in Chicago.

Soon after I left, the house burned to the ground.

The comma in the last sentence is there so the sentence doesn't say *I left the house.*

Commas and direct quotations

Use commas to separate direct quotations from direct references, called attributions, to the speaker.

She said, "I'm going to be late."

"I'll pick up bread," she looked at her list, "and milk."

Use a comma before the attribution, even if the quotation is a complete sentence.

"I have to go to the grocery store," she explained.

Commas and inserted information

Use commas to enclose information inserted into the sentence. Usually this is more important than nonessential information and adds emphasis.

We discussed Christmas bonuses, substantial bonuses, at the meeting.

The chairman of the board indicated everyone, mail clerks to vice presidents, will get a bonus this year.

Commas and direct address

Use commas to enclose nouns or noun phrases used in direct address.

Mr. Potter, may I please have the floor?

I have come to the meeting, coworkers, with sad news.

Commas and nonrestrictive clauses and phrases

Use commas to enclose nonrestrictive clauses and phrases. A nonrestrictive clause or phrase contains information that is not essential to the sentence.

Testing for nonrestrictive clauses and phrases is easy. Read the sentence without the clause or phrase to see if it still says what you mean. If it does, enclose the clause or phrase with commas.

Company profits, from the manufacturing division, will be lower this year.

This sentence says all profits will be lower. It mentions all the company profits come from the manufacturing division.

Company profits from the manufacturing division will be lower this year.

This sentence says the profits from only the company's manufacturing division will be lower. It implies there are other divisions that may not have lower profits.

Commas and omitted words

Sometimes you can omit words in a sentence without confusing the reader. The meaning is still clear from the context. When you do that, a comma indicates words have been left out. This sentence pattern calls for a semicolon in addition to the comma. Here are some examples:

Tammy graduated from Princeton this year; Sarah, Bryn Mawr; Jill, Berkeley.

Todd is our accountant; Susan, controller; Phil, bookkeeper.

I drive an Acura; my brother, a Toyota; my parents, a Buick.

Dash (em-dash) —

The dash is often overused in casual writing. It should be used sparingly in business writing. It is a mark of separation, usually used for greater separation than a comma would give. It is dramatic and a sign of interruption. Be sure that is what you want when you use it.

Use a dash before a final clause if it summarizes what came before.

Cats, dogs, pygmy pigs and birds—her house was full of animals.

Use a dash at the end of a sentence to indicate an interruption or incomplete statement. This happens primarily in dialogue. The dash becomes the final punctuation, so don't use a period, question mark or exclamation point.

"My cat just had kittens, and I was wondering if—"

If the dash is the end of a direct quotation that would normally use a comma before the closing quotation marks, use the comma.

"Are you kidding? My husband would—," she said.

Use dashes to surround words that interrupt the flow of the sentence. Those words may be further explanation of something, an aside said to someone else or a shift of thought.

"You really should see the kittens—they are so adorable—before you say no."

"I don't know if you understand—turn down that television—how much he really doesn't want more pets."

"Would he even notice—no, Kitty, I don't want to pet you right now—one more?"

Uses dashes to surround words or ideas you want to emphasize.

"If you can't find homes for them all—and you'd better try really hard—I'll take one."

Notice there is no space on either side of a dash. Many word processing programs have a special symbol for the dash, instead of the double hyphen (--) we used on typewriters.

Ellipsis . . .

The ellipsis shows that words are deliberately left out of quoted material. Sometimes you don't want or need to quote an entire passage.

"Human minds, at least human minds that are good for much, like to play."

If we only want to use part of that sentence, we show something is missing with an ellipsis.

"Human minds . . . like to play."

Exclamation point !

Exclamation points signal strong emotion or energy. Please be stingy with them. They lose their impact if you use them too frequently. And please, please, don't use more than one at the end of a sentence.

I am so sorry!
Stop it, right now!

Hyphen -

Hyphens combine words into compound words and divide words at the end of a printed line.

Compound words

The *Chicago Manual of Style* says, "Of ten spelling questions that arise in writing or editing, nine are probably concerned with compound words."

So don't feel bad if these give you problems. You are not alone. You will stand out once you know how to handle compound words.

Compound words come in three forms: open, hyphenated and closed. Open compounds are two or more words that stand alone but have meaning as a unit.

floppy disk, soccer mom

Open compounds sometimes turn into hyphenated compounds by common usage.

well-known, acid-rock

Closed compounds started out as two words, but have been condensed to one.

baseball, homemaker

An example of how a word changes over time is *railroad*. First it was written as two words: *rail road*, then it was hyphenated to *rail-road* for awhile, and now we write it as one word. An up-to-date dictionary is the best source for determining which compound forms are acceptable, because they do change.

Here are some general suggestions about hyphenated compounds.

Sometimes when an open compound modifies a noun the meaning is not clear. Hyphenate the compound to avoid confusion.

*A small business man may have trouble
borrowing money.*

If you aren't talking about short guys, you should
hyphenate *small business* so the reader under-
stands *small* belongs to *business* instead of *man.*

*A small-business man may have trouble
borrowing money, no matter how tall he
is.*

Compounds formed with some words—*vice, self,
high, low, all, half, cross*—are hyphenated almost
always.

vice-president
self-esteem
high-priced
low-life
all-inclusive
half-baked
cross-indexed

The word *odd* is always hyphenated with numbers.

50-odd, sixty-odd

Compound numbers from twenty-one to ninety-
nine are hyphenated when written as words.

forty-seven, seventy-nine

Numbers with their unit of measurement are hyphenated only if they precede a noun.

100-meter dash
The race is 100 meters long.

Fractions used as adverbs and adjectives are written as words and hyphenated.

three-quarters finished
but *one third of a yard*

Compounds with *fold* used as adjectives are hyphenated with numerals, but not with numbers written as words.

25-fold increase
but *twofold increase*

Compounds with *best, better, little, well,* etc. are hyphenated if they appear before a noun, unless they are modified by something else.

His well-intentioned gift of cookies caused problems.
My allergy to hickory nuts is little known.
I did get to see the youngest, best looking doctor in the emergency room, though.

Word division

When type is justified (words line up on both the left and right sides), it may be necessary to divide a word at the end of a line. If you use a computer for your writing, most word processing programs handle hyphenation, but they don't all do it well.

You are better off selecting manual hyphenation, so you can decide where words are divided.

The decision where to divide the word is based on syllable division and readability. You don't want to confuse the reader. As the reader's eye moves from one line to the next, you want the first part of the word to give a meaningful clue to the whole word.

Rules and suggestions

The general rule for dividing a word at the end of a line is put the break between syllables. A dictionary will show you where the syllable breaks are if you aren't sure. Here are some suggestions that may save you a trip to the dictionary.

You never divide a single-syllable word. Even if it fits one of the following suggestions, do not divide a single-syllable word. Rewrite the sentence to move that word away from the end of the line, if necessary. Even single-syllable words ending with *-ed* are never hyphenated. Do not divide a word if you would end up with one letter standing alone.

> *alone,* not *a-lone*
> *enough,* not *e-nough*

Don't divide words that would sound different if you pronounced them the way the divided word is written. Many readers silently say the words they are reading, and these words would interrupt the flow of their reading.

women, not *wo-men*

often, not *of-ten* because the *t* is silent

Often a good place to divide a word is between two consonants surrounded by vowels.

foun-dation

struc-ture

Break a word after a vowel.

de-signer

me-nial

If pronunciation indicates a following consonant belongs with the vowel, go for the next vowel.

sepa-rate, not *se-parate*

preju-dice, not *pre-judice*

If the word has two or more vowels in a row, divide after the last in the group.

beau-tiful

poi-son

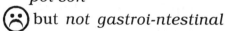 but *not gastroi-ntestinal*

Gastrointestinal would break as *gastro-intestinal,* because it is a compound word. The rules for compound words take precedence over other rules or suggestions.

It is correct to divide a word so there are only two letters on the first line, but avoid division that would put only two letters on the second line.

re-member

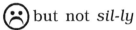 but not *sil-ly*

Compound words formed with hyphens should only be divided at the existing hyphen.

well-informed

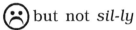 not *well-in-formed*

Compound words without hyphens should be divided so the original words stay intact.

post-master

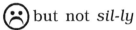 not *postmas-ter*

Words with prefixes should be divided after the prefix.

un-happy

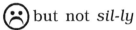 not *unhap-py*

Words that end in *-ing* may be divided so the *ing* goes to the second line. If you doubled the last consonant when you added *-ing,* divide the word between the double consonants.

walk-ing

but *run-ning*

If the original verb ended in *le,* before you added *ing,* divide before the letter preceding the *l.*

    chuc-kling

    crum-bling

Italics *italics*

Italics are the letters that slant to the right a little: *like this.* When we were all using typewriters, and couldn't type italics, the convention of underlining words took hold. In school, you may have learned to underline book titles.

If you write on a computer, you probably can actually italicize words. So don't underline! On a typewriter or in handwritten work, you may still underline anywhere italics should appear.

Italicize punctuation marks at the end of an italicized section, except when the punctuation is not part of an italicized title.

Since the examples in this book are generally written in italics, we need to look at how to deal with italics within italics.

When you need to show italicized items in text that is written in italics, use normal (called roman) type.

    This is how a *book title* appears in a roman type sentence.

> *This is how a* book title *appears in an italic type sentence.*

Just remember the idea is the word should look different from the rest of the sentence.

Italics and titles

Italicize book titles, movie titles, long poem titles, magazine titles, newspaper names, names of works of art and play titles.

We will write these examples differently, so the italics are easier to see.

John Irving's book *A Prayer for Owen Meany* is his best.

The movie based on it is *Simon Birch.*

My father used to faithfully read *Reader's Digest* every month.

It takes about three hours to read the Sunday *New York Times.*

Gretchen's screensaver is an image of the *Mona Lisa.*

Tim's play *Who Are You, and Why Do I Care?* is opening off-Broadway next week.

Have you really read all of Milton's *Paradise Lost*?

Notice the question mark is not part of the title in the last sentence, so it is not italicized.

Italics and foreign words

Foreign words that haven't been absorbed into English should be italicized. Hors d'oeuvres and sauerkraut are two that have been absorbed.

Be careful using foreign words. Resist the urge to use them just to make your writing look educated. Remember the whole idea is to communicate. If you use words your readers don't know, you defeat the whole purpose.

Sometimes the foreign word is the only one that will work, though. Scientific names of animals and plants qualify as foreign words, since they are usually in Latin.

We say a fond *arrivederci* to Rome.

Hasta la vista, baby.

The botanical name for a pansy is *Viola tricolor hortensis.*

Italics for emphasis

Italics can be used to emphasize words, but they should be used sparingly. It is far better to write strong sentences that won't need the help.

Never, I mean *never,* leave a baby alone in the bathtub.

If you *ever* do that again, I'll file charges.

Letters, words and numbers as words

Sometimes you use a letter, word or number as itself, not for what it means. When you do that, italicize the letter, word or number. Have you noticed how many times that occurs in this book? Now you know why.

Scrabble only has one *q* and one *x*.

Please spell *occasion*.

Why is that *4* painted on the house?

When you make plurals of letters, words or numbers used as themselves, the final *s* is not italicized.

Scrabble has twelve *e*'s.

The word list has two *latter*s, but no *later*.

Why are two *5*s painted on the garage?

We talk about plurals of letters and numbers in the apostrophe section of this chapter.

Parentheses ( )

Parenthetical expressions add incidental information to a sentence. If the information is closely related to the rest of the sentence, the expression is set off with commas. If it is less closely related, parentheses are used. Sometimes it is a judgment call whether to use parentheses or dashes. Parentheses are less dramatic than dashes. Expressions within parentheses would probably be said in a slightly different tone of voice in conversation.

My newest client (you met him at the trade show last month) is a pain in the neck.

Punctuation with parentheses

Punctuate the rest of the sentence as though the parentheses were not there. If the parenthetical expression is part of a dependent clause (as this one is), place the comma after the closing parenthesis. In the same way, put the period after the closing parenthesis at the end of a sentence (instead of inside the parentheses).

If the expression within the parentheses is a complete sentence, it should have its own ending punctuation. (Place the parenthetical expression separate from surrounding sentences.)

Use question marks (are you following me so far?) and exclamation points within parentheses if they are called for (I knew you'd catch on!). Notice how the sentence still ends with a period, even with the question mark and exclamation point inside the parentheses.

Parentheses with acronyms

Another important use for parentheses is with acronyms: abbreviations created from the first letters of a series of words. Common acronyms are NATO

(North Atlantic Treaty Organization) and NOW (National Organization for Women).

There are two ways to use parentheses with acronyms. You can either enclose the full name in parentheses right after the first time an acronym appears, or you can enclose the acronym in parentheses right after the full name appears.

After the full name and the acronym appear together, in either order, you can use the acronym alone.

> *When asked about OSHA (Occupational Safety and Health Administration) requirements, the manager seemed hesitant. I wonder if the company complies with OSHA.*
>
> *The Government Printing Office (GPO) is working overtime this weekend. Lights will burn all night at the GPO.*

Parentheses with lists

Parentheses are also used with lists within sentences if you number the items or reference them with letters.

> *The task can be broken down to (1) defining the problem, (2) identifying a solution and (3) tricking our idiot boss into accepting a solution he didn't come up with.*

People are starting to use a single, closing parenthesis for lists, but to be strictly correct either use both opening and closing parentheses or eliminate them entirely.

 1). A single parenthesis is meaningless.

Period .

A period signals the end of an assertion or a command.

The pilot announced the turbulence would last for several minutes.
Please return to your seats.

Abbreviations and periods

Use periods with abbreviations.

Dr.
Ph.D.
U.S.A.

You don't use periods with acronyms.

AFL-CIO
NBA
NASA

Question mark ?

A direct question ends with a question mark.

Are you looking for trouble?

Occasionally you may have a direct question in the middle of a sentence. Use a question mark after the direct question and then continue with the rest of the sentence.

Don't mention the scandal—are you looking for trouble?—at the annual meeting.

Indirect questions do not use question marks.

I asked if you are looking for trouble.

Generally, if the sentence includes the word *ask* it may be an indirect question, so look at it carefully.

A polite question is not really a question; it is a request or command, and it takes a period.

Would you please type this memo.

If your boss has ever said this, you know it isn't a question. It is a request.

Quotation marks " "

Quotation marks enclose direct quotes (either written or spoken) and certain titles.

Direct quotes

Mary said, "If you walk out that door, don't bother coming back."

I told her I'd come back if I wanted to.

The second sentence isn't a direct quote, so it doesn't get quotation marks.

Let's look at those two sentences written another way, so you can clearly see the difference.

Mary said if I walked out the door I shouldn't bother coming back.

I told her, "I'll come back if I want to."

Notice the comma just before the opening quotation mark. If you include an attribution (words like *he said, she cried*), use a comma to set it off from the quotation. You'll need two commas if the attribution is in the middle of the quotation.

"Well, I wondered," he huffed, "if you were going to show up."

If the attribution comes after the direct quotation, the quotation uses a comma before the closing quotation marks—unless the quotation calls for a question mark or exclamation mark.

"Mary should have been home by now," Philip said.

"Did she tell you when she was coming?" he asked.

"I get so worried when she is late!" he said.

Please remember, final commas and periods go inside the quotation marks in common usage.

British usage sometimes puts the comma and period outside the closing quotation mark, but in U.S. usage, the comma and period go inside.

Exclamation points and question marks go outside if they are not part of the quotation.

Did you hear her say, "I'll be 39 in May"?
I wanted to ask, "How many times have you had a 39th birthday?"
I couldn't believe it when he said, "You don't look a day over 35"!
"You are the dearest man!" she said.

Notice that the quotation has no final punctuation of its own when we add the exclamation point and question mark after the quotation marks. It would look awkward to have a period, quotation marks and then still another punctuation mark.

When you quote dialogue, start a new paragraph each time the speaker changes.

Quotes from written material

If the written material you quote has more than one paragraph, use opening quotation marks at the beginning of each paragraph, but use a closing quotation mark only at the end of the last paragraph.

"The mayor was called before the council to answer charges of corruption.
"His attorney advised him to make any and all records available to the public.

> *"The investigation should be complete by the end of the month."*

In formal usage, quotations that are more than eight to ten lines long should be indented on both sides without quotation marks. The indentation tells the reader it is a quotation.

> *I've read that smell is the most evocative of our senses. A scent can trigger stronger memories than a sound or a sight. Music takes me back to another time, especially when the clouds fall on the moon after that third glass of wine. I remember "It's Too Late" from the spring of 1971. Every time I turned on the radio or got into the car, there it was.*

Titles

Quotation marks are also used for titles of short literary works. Use italics for longer works.

Use quotation marks for articles in magazines.

> *He was interviewed in "The 50 Most Powerful Men in America" in this month's* Time.

Use quotation marks for titles of short stories.

> *My favorite Christmas story is "The Gift of the Magi" by O. Henry.*

Use quotation marks for titles of short poems. *We always read "T'was the Night Before Christmas" on Christmas Eve when the kids were little.*

Use quotation marks for titles of chapters in books. *You can find that information in "The Civil War Years" in* A History of America.

Use quotation marks for titles of television shows. Some authorities use italics for the name of a series, with quotation marks reserved for episode titles. If you have the freedom to decide which form you want to use, just be sure you always do it the same way.

I'll call you back after "60 Minutes" is over.

Use quotation marks for titles of radio programs. *He listens to "All Things Considered" on the way home each afternoon.*

Single quotation marks ' '

Single quotation marks are used in place of regular quotation marks if the material is already inside regular quotation marks. This can happen if you have a quotation inside a quotation, or if you use a title within a direct quotation.

My mother said, "I asked your father if he'd loan you the money. He said, 'That kid still hasn't repaid the last loan.' I'll try talking to him again after 'Jeopardy' is over."

As he gave me the book, Bill said, "Be sure to read the chapter 'How to Make a Million Dollars in Your Spare Time.'"

Notice the three quotation marks at the end of the last sentence. That is correct: a single closing quotation mark for the book chapter and then closing double quotation marks for the direct quotation. Even though it is correct, it can look awkward. You may want to avoid that construction. In this case, you could include something more Bill said.

As he gave me the book, Bill said, "Be sure to read 'How to Make a Million Dollars in Your Spare Time.' You'll enjoy it."

If you should need a quotation within a quotation within a quotation, you'd use double quotation marks again. It might be fun to do that, but it can be confusing. It's probably better to find another way to say it without all those levels of quotations.

Semicolon ;

The semicolon is a lovely punctuation mark you just don't see enough. People use commas in many places a semicolon would be proper. Learn to use it correctly and people will be impressed.

A semicolon can join two independent clauses, if you don't use a coordinating conjunction.

Janey slept through her alarm the morning she had an audition; she rushed out with one brown shoe and one black.

You should use a semicolon with conjunctive adverbs (special forms of adverbs used as conjunctions). Place the semicolon before the conjunctive adverb and a comma after it. Some conjunctive adverbs are

also	*moreover*
anyhow	*nevertheless*
consequently	*otherwise*
furthermore	*then*
however	*therefore*

She was a nervous wreck by the time she got to the theater; however, she impressed the director and got the part.

Compound sentences with a lot of internal punctuation (many commas) call for a semicolon, instead of yet another comma, before a conjunction. The semicolon lets the reader know you are leaving one clause and moving on to the next.

With one brown shoe and one black, Janey rushed to the drug store, contract in hand; and she called her agent with the good news.

Use a semicolon to separate a series of items when they are complex or have internal punctuation. While a series usually calls for commas, if you already have several commas you'll need the semicolon to make the separation of items clear.

Next Janey called her mother, who has always supported her dreams; her grandfather, who has sent her money for the last six months; and her high school drama teacher, who had suggested she learn to type.

Pronunciation

People sometimes form opinions of your educational level or intelligence based on how you say the words you use in conversation. While that may be unfair, it is a fact. You probably already knew that, since you are reading this book, eh?

A problem I've encountered is people's mispronouncing words they have seen in print but not heard in conversation. Lots of bright people do it. Years ago I had a high school English teacher who pronounced *epitome* (the ideal example of something) as ep-i-tome, instead of e-pit-o-me.

When you come across a written word you like and think you might want to use, grab the dictionary to check the pronunciation. Say it out loud a couple times as you look at the spelling. Examine how the letters and sound go together. Take a minute right then to save you embarrassment later.

The dictionary entry should show how to divide the word into syllables, which syllable to accent and how to pronounce the word. The pronunciation is written with strange letters like upside-down *e*s and *n*s with tails. The dictionary writers created symbols for all the different sounds the letters and combinations of letters can have. In the front of a good dictionary there should be a section explaining how to use the pronunciation guide. Most dictionaries also have an abbreviated version of the guide at the bottom of the page in the body of the book.

If you have trouble understanding the descriptions of the sounds, try looking up a word you know how to pronounce and see what the pronunciation guide looks like for that word. It may take a little practice, but you will get the hang of it.

Regional differences

Dictionaries offer the pronunciation for unaccented English. If you live in the deep South or New England, you will probably notice some differences in how the dictionary says the word should be pronounced and what you hear your neighbors saying. For instance, in some parts of the South people pronounce car as though as it had an *w* in it: *cawr*. Around Boston, they leave off the *r*: *ca*.

My mother is from New Hampshire, and she used to turn *er* at the end of a word to *a* and *a* to *er*.

Want a glass of wata, Linder?

There is a scene in *My Fair Lady*, where Prof. Higgins identifies where speakers are from in London within a few blocks. Just from their accents. With people all over the country listening to the same nightly news broadcasts and watching the same movies, regional accents are fading.

We won't go into the philosophical question of whether that is a good thing or not. The decision to use regional or standardized pronunciation depends on your needs and goals.

Why English is so tough

English has absorbed enough words from other languages to make general rules for pronunciation impossible. We encounter a similar problem with spelling. This annoys some people. It helps to remember that variety of language makes English rich and versatile.

Accent tip

Here is a tip about words that are pronounced differently when they are used as nouns or verbs. It isn't foolproof, but works most of the time. When the word is used a noun, emphasize the first syllable. When it is working as a verb, emphasize the second syllable.

import

> *He runs an IM-port business.*
> *He im-PORTS ancient artifacts.*

Silent letters

Some letter combinations you don't say as they are written show up more frequently than others. This isn't a complete list, but it does offer some common ones.

gh	night, though	the *gh* is silent
gn	gnat, sign	the *g* is silent
kn	know, knot	the *k* is silent
mb	comb, crumb	the *b* is silent
pn	pneumonia	the *p* is silent
ps	psalm, psychology	the *p* is silent
th	asthma	the *th* is silent
wr	wrap, write	the *w* is silent

Commonly mispronounced words

	Yes	**No**
ask	ask	aks
athlete	ATH-leet	ATH-e-leet
auxiliary	og-ZIL-ye-ree	og-ZIL-ee-air-ee

	Yes	**No**
candidate	KAN-de-date	KAN-a-date
cerebral	se-REE-brel	se-REE-bree-al
environment	en-VI-ren-ment	en-VI-er-ment
et cetera	et-SET-e-re	ek-SET-re
February	FEB-re-wer-ee	FEB-u-air-ee
fiscal	FIS-kel	FIZ-e-kal
genuine	JEN-u-wen	jen-u-INE
impotent	IM-pet-ent	im-PO-tent
integral	INT-e-grel	in-TEG-rel
length	leng(k)th	lenth
mischievous	MIS-che-vis	mis-CHEE-vee-us
picture	PIK-chur	PIT-shur
recognize	REK-ig-nize	REK-er-nize
similar	SIM-e-ler	SIM-u-lur

Elster's Deadly Dozen

Are you guilty of these beastly mispronunciations?

1. Saying nucular for nuclear.

   The correct pronunciation is NOO-klee-ur.

2. Second-syllable stress in preferable and formidable.

   The correct pronunciations are PREF-erable and FOR-midable.

3. Substituting SS for CC in succinct, accessory, succeed, flaccid, etc.

   The double C is properly pronounced like KS or X.

4. Second-syllable stress in influence, affluent and affluence.

   Always stress the first syllable in these words.

5. Pronouncing the *t* in often.

   Do you hear the *t* in soften? It should also be silent in often.

6. Saying kyoopon for coupon.

   Put a coop in it.

7. Saying liberry for library.

   Pronounce that middle R.

8. Saying momento for memento.

   There is no moment in this word. Pronounce it meh-MEN-toh.

9. Erroneous stress on -or- in mayoral, pastoral, pectoral and electoral.

   The proper stress is MAYoral, PAStoral, PECtoral and eLECtoral.

10. Pronouncing height like highth or height-th

    Height should rhyme with night.

11. For forte, meaning "strong point, area of expertise," saying for-TAY.

    The second-syllable accent is wrong. Properly, the word is pronounced in one syllable, like fort, but FOR-tay with first-syllable stress, is now also acceptable.

12. The prissy S in negotiate, controversial and species.

    Make it sh. Say nego-she-ate, controver-shal, spee-sheez.

Contributed by Charles Harrington Elster, author of The Big Book of Beastly Mispronunciations: The Complete Guide for the Careful Speaker *(Houghton Mifflin, 1999) and co-host of "A Way with Words" on San Diego public radio.*

Common Mistakes in English

Spelling

English has borrowed words from many different languages, past and present. That patchwork makes our vocabulary the richest in the world. It also makes spelling hard.

There are many inconsistencies. Words that sound alike often are spelled differently. Words with similar letter patterns are pronounced differently. People complain there are no models to rely on. Well, that's true. Now that we have established that fact, let's get on with making the best of our situation.

We'll offer some rules that will help. We'll list some problem words with hints to remember the proper spelling. If you don't have the gift of spelling, you may have to refer to the dictionary often. Take heart, though. The more you pay attention, the easier it will become. Honest.

It is worth the effort to become a better speller. Nothing destroys your credibility faster than misspelled words. A report with misspelled words means the writer didn't care enough to check for mistakes. Maybe the writer didn't check the facts either.

When you become a better speller, you gain an advantage over people who rely on computer spell-checkers. Spell-checkers can make you look sloppy, because they may not recognize an incorrect word. All they know is if the group of letters make a word. We talk about that in "Confused Words."

Vowels and consonants

Let's talk about how words are built before we get into spelling rules and hints. The letters of the alphabet are divided into vowels and consonants. The vowels are *a, e, i, o, u* and sometimes *y. Y* is a vowel in *shy.* In *play*, it is not. The other letters are all consonants.

Vowels have either a long or short sound. The long sound is the same as the name of the letter. Here are some examples of words with long vowel sounds:

    bait, beet, bite, boat, butte

The short sounds are not as easy to illustrate, because there is often more than one for each vowel. Here are a few of the common short sounds:

    bat, bet, bit, bought, but

Most of the consonant sounds are obvious. Some of the less obvious ones are covered in "Pronunciation."

Syllables

Words can be divided into syllables. A syllable is the smallest package of sound in the word. Letters have sounds, but they blend together in words. If you are musical, think of how many beats a word has to count syllables. In most words, one syllable is stressed, or accented, more than the others.

Examples will work better than explanation. Here are some words divided into syllables with the stressed syllable written in all uppercase letters.

CON-cen-trate
re-spon-si-BIL-i-ty
AU-to-mo-bile
pro-MO-tion

Spelling rules

These rules are not always true. I'm sorry. They can help, though. As you encounter the exceptions they may jump out at you, so you are more apt to remember them.

Words with *ei* and *ie*

As a child, you may have learned the rhyme, "*I* before *E*, except after *C*." Add, "and in words like eight, where it sounds like *A*," and you've got a good start on mastering this combination.

I before *E*
  achieve
  piece
  grief

except after *C*
  ceiling
  receive
  receipt

sounds like *A*
  beige
  neighbor
  weigh

Here are some common exceptions and hints to remember which letter comes first. Feel free to make up your own if these are too weird for you!

caffeine	Coffee has an E.
either	If you say ee-ther, it is easy to remember. If you say i-ther, it is harder.
height	HE has more height than I.
protein	Meat has lots of protein, and meat has an E.
seize	Seize the sneeze. (This is a dangerous one, I admit. You might want to spell it seeze!)
sheik	She loved the SHEik
weird	We are WEird.

Double or single *l* ?

Words that end in *-ful* take one *l*.

beautiful

wonderful

awful

When you add the suffix *-ly*, you will end up with two *l*s. Remember you started with only one *l*.

Words with *-ally* always have two *l*s).

Finally, occasionally, usually

When to double

Here is a rule about doubling the last letter in a word when you add suffixes that start with a vowel: *-ing*, *-ed*, *-er*, *-est*, for example.

Double the last letter if it is a single consonant (except *x*) coming after a single vowel in a single syllable word. It isn't as complicated as that sounds.

Shop, shopping, shopped

(one syllable, last letter is a single consonant coming after a single vowel)

look, looking, looked

(one syllable, last letter is single consonant but there are two vowels before the last letter—so don't double)

The same rule applies to words with more than one syllable, if the last syllable is stressed. If the accent is on the last syllable, double the last letter (except *x*) if it is a single consonant coming after a single vowel. This isn't as easy as the single syllable words, because some words are not strongly accented. You can always check the dictionary if you aren't sure.

embed, embedding, embedded
refer, referring, referred

Sometimes when you add the suffix, the stress or accent moves to the first syllable of the word. If that happens, do not double the final consonant.

refer, reference

Words that end in *-gram* always double the m when you add suffixes.

program, programming, programmer

Exceptions

The letter *q* is always followed by a *u* in English words. This combination is considered a consonant for the doubling rule. The word *quit* fits the rule if we consider *qu* as a consonant.

quit, quitter, quitting

Three compound words that end in *p* always double the *p* when adding a suffix.

handicap, handicapped, handicapping
kidnap, kidnapped, kidnapping
worship, worshipped, worshipping

Dropping the e

Sometimes the final *e* of a word disappears when you add *-ing* and *-ed*. Here is a pretty solid rule for that.

If the word ends in a silent *e*, drop it before you add *-ing* and *-ed*.

Shape, shaping, shaped

Words that end in *-ce* and *-ge* preserve the *e* before *-able*, *-ous* and *-ment*.

Management, courageous, noticeable (judgment is the exception)

Words that end in o

If word ends in *o* with a consonant right before it, you usually add *-es* to make the plural.

echo	*echoes*
potato	*potatoes*
torpedo	*torpedoes*
veto	*vetoes*

If the *o* doesn't have a consonant right before it, just add *s* to make the plural.

radio	*radios*
tattoo	*tattoos*

Odd plurals

There are some words that don't follow any rules for plurals. I'll bet you already know most of them.

appendix	*appendices*
child	*children*
goose	*geese*
louse	*lice*
man	*men*
mouse	*mice*
ox	*oxen*
radius	*radii*
sheep	*sheep*
tooth	*teeth*

I don't know how often you use the word *mongoose*, but just in case you need to know: it doesn't come from the same source as *goose*. So the plural is *mongooses*.

Changing y to *i*

Words that end in *y* keep the *y* before *-ing*.

Try, trying, tried

Words that end in *y* change the *y* to *i* before *-ness* and *-ly*.

Lazy, laziness, lazily

When you add other suffixes, including adjectives *-er* and *-est* endings, to a word ending in *y*, look at the letter just before the *y*. If that next to the last letter is a vowel, keep the *y*. If the letter right before the *y* is a consonant, change the *y* to an *i*.

sky, skies

day, days

study, studied

play, played

happy, happier, happiest

coy, coyer, coyest

Adjectives to adverbs

When you change an adjective that ends in *-le* to an adverb with the *-ly* form, just change the *e* to a *y*.

bubble	*bubbly*
double	*doubly*
simple	*simply*

Adding prefixes

Do not drop or double any letters when you add a prefix. Just stick the prefix right in front of the word.

disagree, but *misspell*

unexciting, but *unnecessary*

Learn common word patterns

Here are some word patterns you encounter almost every day.

-eau

beauty

bureaucrat
chateau
tableau

-eigh

height
neigh
sleigh
weigh

-ight

light
might
bright
sight

-sion

incision
precision
suspension
tension

-tion

action
infection
nation
station

-ounce

bounce

flounce
ounce
pounce

The building blocks

Learning some common suffixes and prefixes will help with spelling. If you master these building blocks, you have a head start on many of the longer words in English.

Prefixes

A prefix is a syllable added at the beginning of a word to add to or change its meaning. Many of our common prefixes come from the Greek (G) and Latin (L). Recognizing these prefixes and knowing their meaning will expand your spelling skills tremendously.

a- (G) not, without (usually used with a consonant other than *h*)
amoral, asexual

ab- (L) away; from
abduct (duct means to lead: air conditioning ducts lead the air), absent (-sent is a form of the Latin verb to be, so absent is to be away)

ac- (L) to (usually used before c, k or q)
  accompany, acknowledge

ad- (L) to (usually used before letters other than c, f, k, l, p, q, s and t)
  adapt (apt means fit), adopt (opt means choose)

aer(o)- (G) air
  aerobics, aerosol

af- (L) to (usually used before f)
  affix, afflict (-flict comes a Latin word meaning strike. To be afflicted with a disease is to be struck by it.)

agr- (G) field
  agriculture, agrochemical

al- (L) to (usually used before l)
  allure, alleviate (al-leviate means to make light and is related to levitate and levity)

ambi- (L) both; double
  ambidextrous

amphi- (G) both
  amphibious

an- (G) not, without (usually used with a vowel and sometimes *h*)
  anaerobic, anarchy (archy means ruler: no ruler in anarchy)

ana- (G) backward

anachronism (chron means time: an anach-
ronism is something not in the time it be-
longs), anagram (gram means letter:
anagrams are jumbled letters—maybe back-
wards?)

ante- (L) before

anteroom, antecedent (cede means to go:
an antecedent goes before)

anti- (G) against

anticlimax, antibiotic

ap- (L) to (usually used before p)

appear (pear comes from a word that means
show oneself), apprehend (prehend means
seize)

arch- (G) chief, extreme

archenemy, archconservative

as- (L) to (usually used before s)

assign (sign means mark: when you as-
sign something to a person you make it
his), associate (sociate means join; social
comes from the same word)

at- (L) to (usually used before t)

attest (test comes from a word that means
witness: when you attest, you swear it is

true), attract (tract means to draw; same root for contract, distract and detract)

be- cause to be
belittle, bewitch

bi- (L) two
bipolar, bicycle

circum- (L) round
circumnavigate, circumvent (vent comes from a word that means come: to circumvent means make a circuit around)

co- (L) together
cooperate, coworker

col- (L) together (usually used before *l*)
collect (lect comes from a word that means gather), collapse (lapse means to slip, fall)

com- (L) together (usually used before *b*, *m* and *p*)
combine (bine comes from a word that means two by two. Notice the bi- which means two?), companion (panion comes from a word that means bread or food. Isn't this fun?), comprehend (prehend means sieze: sieze together could mean putting it all together)

con- (L) together (usually used before sounds other than *b*, *l*, *m* and *p*) concentrate (*centrate comes from a word that means center; when you concentrate you bring things together to a common center*), conclave (*clave comes from word that means key; a conclave is a private meeting. Maybe behind locked doors?*)

contra- (L) against
contradict (*dict means to speak*), contrary

cor- (L) together
correct (*rect comes from a word that means to lead straight: to lead straight together can mean doing something the right way*), corrugate (*rogate comes from a word that means wrinkle*)

counter- (L) against
counterbalance, counterrevolutionary

de- do the opposite, reduce, remove
deactivate, devalue, dethrone

dia- (G) through, across
diagram (*gram means writing: a diagram gives information through writing*), dialogue (*logue relates to speaking: dialogue gives information through speaking*)

dis- (L) not
disagree, disconnect

e- (L) out, from
  evolve, emerge

ex- (L) out, former
  excommunicate, ex-president

extra- (L) beyond
  extrasensory (beyond the five senses), extraterrestrial (beyond earth)

hemi- (G) half
  hemisphere (half a circle; often half the earth)

hydro- (G) water
  hydroelectric, hydrology (the study of water)

hyper- (G) above, over
  hyperactive, hypersensitive

hypo- (G) under
  hypodermic (under the skin), hypocrite (literally it means someone who under-judges; perhaps a person not critical enough with himself: one who allows himself to not live up to the ideals he says he believes in)

il- (L) not (usually used before *l*)
  illogical, illiterate

im- (L) in, into (usually used before *b, m* or *p*)
  immigrate (migrate means to move)

im- (L) not (usually used before *b*, *m* or *p*)
  impossible (not possible), immovable (not movable)

in- (L) in, into (usually used before sounds other than *b*, *l*, *m*, *p* or *r*)
  inbreed, inquire (quire means to seek: inquire means to seek into or investigate)

in- (L) not (usually used before sounds other than *b*, *l*, *m*, *p* or *r*)
  incredible, innocent (nocent comes from a word that means noxious or harmful: innocent means not wicked)

inter- (L) between
  intermediate (mediate comes from a word that means middle: something that is intermediate is in the middle between other things), intersect (sect comes from a word that means cut: intersect means to cut between)

intro- (L) within
  introspection (spection comes from a word that means look: introspection means looking within yourself), introduce (duce comes from the word duct which means to lead: when you introduce someone to something new, you lead them into it)

ir- (L) not (usually used before *r*)
  irregular, irresponsible

log-, logo- (G) word, reason
  logo, logic (comes from the word for reason)

mal- *(L) bad*
  maladjusted, malfunction

met-, meta- (G) change
  metamorphosis (morph means shape: metamorphosis means change shape. Remember the caterpillar and the butterfly?)

mis- wrong
  misinformation, mispronounce

non- (L) not
  nonconformist, nonscheduled

ob- (L) in the way of
  obstruct (struct means to build: obstruct means to build in the way of or interfere with); obliterate (literate comes from a word that means letter: obliterate means to get in the way of the letters, make something unreadable. In common usage it means to totally remove from memory.)

per- (L) thoroughly, through

perennial (ennial means annual: perennial means present through the year), perforate (forate comes from a word that means to bore a hole: perforate means make a hole through something)

peri- (G) all around
periscope (scope means see: look all around with a periscope), perimeter (meter means measure: perimeter is a boundary, what you would measure all around)

post- (L) after
postgraduate (after graduation), postscript (after writing: words at the end of a letter or article. P.S. means postscript)

pre- (L) before
precede (cede means to go; pre means before: precede means go before), precognition (cognition means to know; precognition is a premonition, to know something before it happens)

pro- (L) forward
proceed (ceed is a form of cede, which means to go: proceed means go forward), promote (mote means to move: promote means move ahead)

re- (L) back, again

    recede (cede means go; re means back. Recede means go back. Think of a receding hair line!), recline (cline means to bend: recline means to bend backwards)

retro- (L) backward

    retrospective (spect means look at: retrospective means look back at. When a famous person dies, someone always does a retrospective to look back at his life.)

se- (L) aside, apart

    secede (cede means go; se means apart. When the Southern states seceded—went apart—from the Union, we ended up with the Civil War.)

semi- (G) half, not complete

    semiautomatic (not completely automatic)

sub- (L) under

    subterranean (terra means earth; sub means under. Subterranean means under the ground. Think of a subterranean cave.)

super- (L) extra

    superhuman (A superhuman feat is more than a regular person could do.)

sur- (L) over

surcharge (A surcharge is a charge on top of, or over, another charge.)

sym- (G) together
sympathy (pathy means feeling; sym means together; sympathy means feeling together. When you have sympathy for someone, you feel with them.)

syn- (G) together
synchronous (chrono means time; syn means together; ous means a state of being. Synchronous means being at the same time. Think of synchronized swimming.)

trans- (L) beyond, across
transport (port means carry—think of portable; trans means across. Transport means carry across.)

un- opposite
unlikely (This one's not very interesting. That happens when you get away from the Greek and Latin words.)

uni- one
uniform (form means shape; uni means one. Uniform means one shape. Think of uniforms that people wear to look alike. Also, if you describe something as being uniform, you mean it is all the same.)

I bet you didn't realize how much Greek and Latin you know! Looking at the pieces of words can help you figure out words you don't know, as well as improve your spelling.

Suffixes

A suffix is a syllable added to the end of a word to add to or change the word's meaning.

-able capable of
  knowledgeable

-ance act of, state of
  performance

-ancy act of, state of
  pregnancy

-ate make, perform the act of
  decorate

-ate having
  affectionate

-ation act of, state of
  investigation

-dom state of
  freedom

-ed having
  two-legged

-eer doer
   profiteer

-en make, perform the act of
   sharpen

-ence act of, state of
   occurrence

-ency act of, state of
   presidency

-er doer (usually male or unspecified)
   painter

-ery act of, state of
   bravery

-ess doer (usually female)
   poetess

-ful full of
   colorful

-fy make, perform the act of
   magnify

-hood act of, state of
   motherhood

-ible capable of
   collectible

-ic, ical resembling
   musical

-ice act of, state of
  cowardice

-ion act of, state of
  production

-ish resembling
  brutish

-ism act of, state of
  communism

-ist doer
  terrorist

-ive having
  productive

-ize, -ise make, perform the act of
  visualize

-less without
  careless

-like resembling
  childlike

-ly resembling
  manly

-ment act of, state of
  government

-ness act of, state of
  laziness

-or doer (usually male or unspecified)
  actor

-ous (L) full of
  poisonous

-ress, doer *(usually female)*
  temptress

-ship act of, state of
  friendship

-sion act of, state of
  persuasion

-tion act of, state of
  reduction

-ular (L) resembling
  circular

-ulent (L) full of
  fraudulent

Combining forms

Combining forms are bases meant to combine with either another combing form or a word.

anthropo- (G) human being
  anthropology, anthropomorphic

-arch (G) ruler, leader
  monarch

archae- (G) ancient
　　archaeology

auto- (G) self
　　autograph, autobiography

bene- good
　　benefactor, benediction

bi-, bio- life
　　biology, biosphere

biblio- (G) book
　　bibliography, bibliophile

-cide kill
　　pesticide, suicide (*sui* is from the Latin and
　　means *oneself*)

-cracy form of government
　　theocracy, democracy

-crat advocate
　　technocrat, democrat

dema-, demo- (G) people
　　demagogue, democracy

eu- (G) good
　　eugenic, eulogy

-gamy (G) marriage
　　bigamy, monogamy

ge-, geo- (G) earth
geography, geology

geno- (G) race
genocide

-gen (G) producer
antigen, pathogen

-gram (G) drawing, writing
sonogram, telegram

-graph (G) writing
telegraph, autograph

heter-, hetero- (G) different
heterosexual, heterogeneous

hom-, homo- (G) alike
homosexual, homogenized

-log, -logue (G) talk
dialogue, monologue

-logy (G) study
theology, biology

macr-, macro- (G) large
macroeconomics, macroscopic

mal- (L) bad
malcontent, malnourished

meg-, mega- (G) large, million
megaphone, megabyte

-metry (G) measurement
  *telemetry, geometry (literally earth mea-
  surement, geometry was invented by the
  Egyptians to measure their fields)*

micr-, micro- (G) small
  microscope, microchip

mon-, mono- (G) one, lone
  monogamy, monologue

-morph, -morphic, -morphus, -morphy (G) having
such a form
  polymorph

multi- (L) many
  multifaceted, multicultural

neur-, neuro- (G) nerve
  neurology, neurotransmitter

omni- (L) all
  omnipresent, omnivorous

-opsy (G) examination
  biopsy

path-, patho- (G) disease
  pathology, pathologist

-path (G) practitioner of a system of medicine, or
a sufferer of a disorder
  homeopath, psychopath

-pathy (G) feeling
    sympathy, antipathy

pan-, pant-, panto- (G) all
    pantomime, pandemic

phil-, philo- (G) lover
    philanthropy, philosophy

-phil, -phile (G) loving
    bibliophile, pedophile

phon-, phono- (G) sound
    phonograph, phonology

-phone (G) sound
    telephone, homophone

phot-, photo- (G) light
    photon, photograph

poly- (G) many
    polygon, polygamy

pseud-, pseudo- (G) false
    pseudoscience, pseudosophisticated

psych-, psycho- (G) the mind
    psychologist, psychopath

self- of oneself
    self-closing, self-taught

-scope (G) means of viewing

telescope, microscope

-sophy (G) knowledge, wisdom
philosophy (literally means love of knowledge)

tel-, tele- (G) distant
telephone, telephoto

the-, theo- god
theism, theology

-vorous (L) eating
omnivorous, herbivorous

Commonly misspelled words

Here are some commonly misspelled words with room to write tips to remember them.

absence

accept

accessible

accommodate

accompany

accomplishment

accurate

acknowledgment

acquaintance

advertisement

affluence

agreeing

agreement

amateur

analysis

analyze

anniversary

apologize

apparent

appearance

apprehensible

argument

association

assurance

athletic

audible

awful

awkward

bachelor

balance

battalion

beginning

benefited

bicycle

bookkeeper

bridge

business

candidate

carriage

cemetery

changeable

column

commendable

commission

committee

competent

confidence

conscience

conscientious

conscious

contrivance

convenience

comprehensible

correspondence

correspondent

curriculum

definite

dependent

deplorable

description

desperate

develop

development

dining

disagreeable

discipline

diseases

disparate

durable

eighth

embarrassing

endurance

equivalent

especially

excellence

existence

familiar

fantasy

fascinating

February

fiery

fifth

finally

forcible

foreign

forty

friend

generally

genius

grammar

grateful

grievance

guard

gullible

handle

height

hoping

humorous

illegible

imaginable

imitation

immutable

indelible

independent

innocence

intelligence

interfere

interrupt

invitation

irresistible

judgment (judgement is an alternative spelling)

knowledge

labeled

laboratory

laudable

lightning

literally

literature

livelihood

loneliness

lose

loyalty

magazine

maintenance

malleable

marriage

mathematics

miniature

minutes

misspelled

musician

mysterious

naturally

necessary

neither

nickel

niece

ninety

noticeable

oblige

occasion

occur

occurrence

omission

omitted

operate

opinion

opportunity

optimistic

opulence

original

owing

panicked

parallel

paralyzed

parliament

particular

pastime

peaceable

permanent

perishable

permissible

perseverance

persistence

personally

persuade

physically

piece

planning

pleasant

politics

portrayed

possession

possible

prairie

preceding

predominance

preference

prejudice

preparation

presence

preponderance

privacy

privilege

probably

professor

prominence

pronunciation

prophecy

proved

psychology

quarter

quiet

receipt

receive

recommend

reference

referred

referring

reliance

relieve

religious

repetition

reprehensible

representative

respectability

respectfully

restaurant

responsible

rhythm

sacrifice

scene

schedule

secretary

seize

sentence

separate

sergeant

severely

sincerely

sophomore

source

strength

succeed

superintendent

suspicion

sustenance

surely

surprise

technical

temperament

temperature

tendency

thorough

tolerance

tractable

tragedy

transferred

truly

twelfth

Common Mistakes in English

until

unconscious

university

until

unusual

valuable

vegetable

violence

village

villain

weather

Wednesday

weird

whether

wonderful

writing

written

Confused Words

I heard a young mother talking about taking her coughing baby to the doctor: "He said she had ammonia." I'm pretty sure the doctor actually said *pneumonia.* While I enjoyed listening to the rest of her conversation, I couldn't take any of it seriously. That's a shame, because she might have had something useful to say about sick children. I simply couldn't trust her skill at communicating what she knew.

If you want people to pay attention to what you say and write, you must use words correctly.

Your computer spell checker won't help you with these words. It only looks for a collection of letters that aren't arranged correctly. If the letters spell a word, the spell checker's job is done. It can't tell you if that is the word you meant to use.

The following words are frequently confused with each other. The confusion can start because they seem alike. People may hear or read a word that sounds or looks like a word they are familiar with and then use it without noticing it isn't quite the right word.

Other times people don't know two words that sound exactly the same are spelled differently and have different meanings. Those words are called homonyms. *Reel* and *real* are good examples. Homonyms don't cause any problems when you speak, but they do jump out at the reader when you write the incorrect one.

Still other words seem to say almost the same things. Many of them may work when you talk to family or friends, but will signal your lack of language skill when you have a conversation with a stranger.

The list I've made and your dictionary can help you chose the correct word. As you read the list, think about words you hear other people misuse.

By the way, correcting anyone besides your children is a sure fire way to become very unpopular! Using correct language can be contagious, though. As your word choices become more accurate and precise, folks around you may notice and decide they need to clean up their acts.

I have left room for you to add words that cause you trouble. If you think you may be using a word incorrectly, check the dictionary for the correct spelling and pronunciation and add it to the list.

Make it a game with your kids to give them a head start in language.

accept: receive
except: other than
They accept deliveries every day except Sunday.

addition: the result of adding
edition: the form in which something is presented
With the addition of a morning edition, the newspaper expanded the news coverage

advice: (noun) recommendation
advise: (verb) recommend
I would advise you to take his advice.

affect: (v) influence
(There is a noun form of *affect*, but it is primarily used in psychology.)
effect: (v) bring about; (n) result
Losing her job affected her vacation plans. Being rude to her boss effected an unsatisfactory evaluation. The effect was her being fired.

aggravate: make worse
irritate: annoy
Irritating Grandpa aggravates his bad mood.

The common usage distinction between *irritate* and *aggravate* is quickly fading.

aisle: passage
isle: island
> *He hogged the aisle seat on our flight to the tropical isle.*

all ready: completely ready
already: previously
> *You already told me you were all ready.*

allusion: an indirect reference
delusion: something falsely believed
illusion: something that misleads
> *I didn't understand his allusion to the Bible.*
> *He is under the delusion that he's getting a promotion.*
> *The magician's illusions were unbelievable.*

all together: everyone in one place
altogether: completely, on the whole
> *Getting the entire family all together was not altogether a good idea.*

all ways: every method
always: forever; at all times
> *All ways to the lake are always busy on Friday afternoon.*

allude: make an indirect reference to

elude: evade

Did you allude to your problem, or did you come out and tell him?

If you have nothing to hide, why would you try to elude the police?

apathetic: showing no feeling
pathetic: deserving pity

The fans have become so apathetic, they don't even notice a good play.

I feel sorry for the pathetic team since they lost their only good player.

altar: part of a church
alter: change

You cannot alter the candles on the altar without the priest's permission.

amoral: beyond the scope of moral judgment
immoral: not ethical

Scientific knowledge is amoral: it isn't right or wrong—it just exists.

Using scientific knowledge to harm people is immoral.

amount: used with things that are not counted
number: used with things that are counted

We got a large amount of snow last night.

A large number of snow plows are working today.

anxious: worried
eager: full of impatient desire
I am eager to start my new job, but anxious about all the additional responsibilities.

any one: any thing
anyone: any person
Anyone who has trouble hearing may take any one of the front seats.

apt to: suited by nature
liable to: vulnerable
likely to: probably
These three words are used almost interchangeably now.

Cactus are apt to survive much neglect.
Plants are liable to die, if they are watered too much.
You are likely to kill plants, especially cactus, if you water them too much.

as: in the way or manner (used before a phrase or clause)
like: in the same way (used before a noun or pronoun)
This is another example of fading differences. Now

days lots people use *like* before a phrase or clause as often as they do with a noun or pronoun. There are even some authorities who say that is acceptable. You won't go wrong by following this rule, though.

> *He was polite, as I hoped he would be.*
> *He was polite like a good boy.*

bad: adjective
badly: adverb

> *That was a really bad game.*
> *The pitcher threw badly from the first inning.*
> *I felt bad for all the people who sat through the game.*

Resist the temptation to say you "felt badly for all the people." To *feel badly* means you didn't do a very good job of feeling. In the example above, *bad* is an adjective that refers to the subject of the sentence—*I.*

bazaar: a fair, originally an oriental market
bizarre: strikingly out of the ordinary

> *If you want to see some bizarre handicrafts, check out the bazaar at the beach.*

berth: a place for a ship; a bed
birth: being born

> *Mrs. Schwartz gave birth in the upper berth while the ship was at berth.*

beside: next to

besides: other than

> *The waiter flirted with the pretty girls beside me.*

In this sentence he flirted with the girls next to me. I'm not saying whether I am pretty or not.

> *The waiter flirted with the pretty girls besides me.*

Here he flirted with all the pretty girls except me, and I am one of the pretty girls.

boar: male pig

boor: rude, uncouth person

bore: tiresome, uninteresting person

> *This boar won big at the National Pig Show.*
> *I always avoid that boor from accounting because of his crude language.*
> *My mind always wanders when I'm speaking with the bore from shipping.*

brake: slow down or stop

break: damage or destroy

> *If you don't add more fluid before the trip, your brake may break.*

bridal: related to brides or weddings

bridle: (n) part of horse headgear; (v) restrain

> *Try to bridle your frustration over the horse's ill-fitting bridle as the bridal party passes*

*by, so your ugly mood won't spoil the wed-
ding.*

bring: carry toward
take: carry away
*Please bring me the Jones file, and take
this memo to the receptionist.*

callus: hard thickened area of skin
callous: uncaring
*My doctor removed the callus on my foot
without offering me any anesthesia.
His callous attitude hurt me as much as
the physical pain.*

can: physically able
may: have permission
*You can not walk on water, but you may
go swimming.*

canvas: tightly woven cloth used for sails, clothes
and tents; cloth to paint on
canvass: go through a district to ask for votes or
determine opinions
*Wear your canvas shoes when we canvass
the neighborhood.*

capital: seat of government; related to money;
uppercase letter
capitol: building where government does business
(capitalized for the building Congress meets in)

My grandmother usually lives on her investment interest, but her trip to the nation's capital cost so much she dipped into her capital last month.

She said seeing the Capitol, where her grandfather served as a senator, was worth every penny.

carat: unit of weight for precious stones
caret: mark (^) to indicate where something should be inserted
carrot: root vegetable

Her engagement ring is an obscene two-carat diamond.

A proofreader will put a missing comma under a caret.

Any really good stew has to have lots of carrots, as well as onions and potatoes.

cast: actors in a play; support for broken bone
caste: social division

During the previous century, the Vanderbilts were of a higher caste than the cast of a travelling musical comedy.

censer: vessel for burning incense
censor: (v) examine for objectionable matter; (n) one who censors
censure: official reprimand

sensor: device that senses

The priest swung the censer as he walked up the aisle.

A censor read each letter to make sure it didn't contain any military secrets.

The Senate can censure the President if a majority of Senators think he did something bad enough.

The motion sensor alerted the museum guards to an intruder.

cereal: a grain, often eaten at breakfast

serial: arranged in or belonging to a series

The serial killer ate cereal for breakfast.

cession: act of yielding

session: a meeting; time period

To show good faith, management made the cession of agreeing to let labor pick the place for the next bargaining session.

cite: quote

sight: function of seeing

site: a place

I would cite the source of my information, if I could remember it.

You are a sight for sore eyes.

The building site has been approved.

climatic: relating to climate

climactic: relating to a climax

> *The climatic change that melted all the polar ice caps and flooded most of the world was a climactic ending to the movie.*

clothes: articles of clothing

cloths: pieces of fabric

> *Put on your clothes and we'll go buy some dishcloths.*

coarse: rough

course: path or route

> *The coarse grass on the golf course made putting difficult.*

core: center

corps: body of people

> *If you could see inside any member of the Marine Corps, you would see a core of pride and discipline.*

collaborate: work with

corroborate: support

> *I would love to collaborate with you on the project.*
>
> *My story will be more believable if you corroborate it by saying you were with me.*

compliment: a flattering comment

complement: to complete or go with

I blushed when he complimented my perfect grammar.

Chocolate ice cream complements any meal.

consul: government representative in a foreign country
council: governing body
counsel: advice; consultant

I have an appointment tomorrow to speak with the Brazilian consul about that country's extradition laws.

The City Council is investigating corruption in my department.

My legal counsel told me not to answer any questions unless she is with me.

confidant: someone you share secrets with
confident: certain

Are you confident you can trust your confidant with that juicy tidbit?

conscience: sense of right and wrong
conscious: aware

My conscience bothers me because I wasn't conscious of your pain.

contemptible: deserving scorn
contemptuous: feeling or expressing contempt

Your contemptible behavior made me contemptuous of you.

continual: in steady succession

continuous: without interruption

   That dog barks continually.

It only seems that he barks continuously!

   Your heart beats continuously.

could have: this is the proper form

could of: WRONG

   I could have danced all night.

credible: believable

credulous: ready to believe, without good reason

   He is so credulous he will accept any rea-
   son, even if it isn't credible.

cue: a signal; a stick used in pool and billiards

queue: a waiting line (also a long braid of hair,
but you seldom see that use)

   Cue the pool player with the cue in his
   hand to please stand in the queue for the
   rest room.

currant: type of raisin

current: up to date; fast moving water; flow of
electricity

   Baking recipes of a hundred years ago used
   more currants than current ones do.

cymbal: brass plate that produces a clashing tone
when hit

symbol: something that stands for something else

The man who plays the cymbal at the end of the symphony could be a symbol for all part-time workers.

decimate: destroy a large part (originally one-tenth of the whole, but common usage has changed it)

disseminate: spread throughout

The king's herald disseminated the news that the army had been decimated.

decent: worthwhile

descent: move downward

dissent: difference of opinion

He was a decent guy with some bad luck.

His financial descent put him on the streets.

His dissent with his family stopped him from asking for their help.

decry: strongly disapprove

descry: catch sight of

If my parents descry my daughter's boy-friend with the pierced lip, they will decry a whole generation's standards.

deprecate: disapprove of

depreciate: lower the value of

His deprecating remarks about my behavior made me angry.

The minute you drive a new car off the lot it depreciates by thousands of dollars.

detract: take away something
distract: draw away attention

I don't like to detract from his presentation, but the misspelled words on the slides did distract my attention from the important information.

device: piece of equipment for a specific use
devise: invent

He devised a nifty device to flatten your belly.

dew: moisture
do: perform
due: because of; owed

The morning dew glistened on my freshly-washed car.

Do me a favor and wash the car.

Due to my being out of work, I couldn't pay the rent when it was due.

die: stop living
dye: color

That plant will die if you don't start watering it.

My grandmother used to dye stained clothes a darker color and make us wear them.

different from: this the proper form

different than: WRONG

The man I saw her with last night is different from the one she brought to the Christmas party.

disapprove: not approve
disprove: show to be false

My rabbi disapproves of the movements trying to disprove the Holocaust.

disinterested: impartial
uninterested: not interested

I am disinterested in the disagreement, so I will mediate and help solve it.
I am uninterested in the disagreement, so I will go talk to someone else.

dual: double
duel: combat between two people

After his dual insult of seducing my wife and bragging about it, I had to challenge him to a duel.

elicit: draw out
illicit: unlawful

If you can elicit a confession from her, we may be able to shut down the illicit operation.

emulate: imitate

immolate: kill, usually as a sacrifice

The missionaries convinced the natives to stop emulating their ancestors by immolating young girls.

emigrant: one who leaves a country

immigrant: one who enters a country

He is an emigrant from Switzerland.

He is an immigrant to this country.

A person is both an emigrant and immigrant. People emigrate from one county before they immigrate to another. Remember the **E**migrant comes before **I**mmigrant.

eminent: important

imminent: soon

The imminent arrival of the eminent statesman has closed all the downtown streets.

epaulet (or epaulette): fringed shoulder pad, part of military uniform

epitaph: inscription on a grave

epithet: abusive word or phrase

The gold on the military band member's epaulet glistened in the afternoon sun.

He read the epitaph on his commanding officer's grave.

He screamed an epithet at an unjust god and walked away.

every one: each person or thing
everyone: all people
> *Every one of us could make life easier for everyone if we were more polite.*

exercise: exertion; use
exorcise: expel
> *Hard exercise can exorcise demon tension.*

expand: enlarge
expend: spend
> *If you expand your horizons and expend more energy, you might meet your goals.*

expect: look forward
suspect: distrust
suppose: imagine
> *"I suppose you suspect me of eating the last cookie," he said as he brushed crumbs off his chest. "I expected you would."*

explicit: fully expressed
implicit: implied
> *If you don't complain about the sexually explicit advertising, you give your implicit approval of it.*

facility: aptitude; something built for a particular purpose
faculty: ability; teaching staff

The faculty at this facility seems to have a faculty to foster the students' facilities.

fair: impartial; gathering of buyers/sellers
fare: charge for travel; food
   The reporter wrote a fair review of the book fair, even though I refused to pay his air fare and he didn't like the fare at the cookbook booth.

farther: a greater distance
further: to a greater degree
   If we continue to move farther from guidelines, we won't make further progress with this project.

feat: act of skill, ingenuity or endurance
feet: more than one foot
   Juggling while riding a unicycle 12 feet tall is quite a feat.

fewer: not as many (things you can count)
less: not as much (things you cannot count)
   We'd have fewer arguments if you spent less time on the Internet.
   We'd have less unhappiness if you spent fewer hours on the Internet.

find: encounter
fined: imposed a fine

I was surprised to find your car parked in the red zone, since you were fined for that last week.

flair: skill or style
flare: blaze up
My neighbor has quite a flair with food. From across the street, I can see her flaming cherries jubilee flare.

flammable: able to burn
inflammable: able to burn
These two words mean the same thing. Isn't English fun? The word for things that don't burn is *nonflammable.*

flaunt: display to public view
flout: scorn
She flaunts her beauty and flouts any criticism of her behavior.

floe: floating sheet of ice (*ice floe* is the common usage)
flow: move in a stream
The ice floe is flowing down the river straight for the dam.

forbear: restrain
forebear: ancestor

Please forbear your irritation tonight if he starts bragging about his forebears who came over on the Mayflower.

foreword: preface to a book
forward: toward the front
Since the foreword should appear before the table of contents, you will have to move those pages forward.

formally: in a formal manner
formerly: previously
I would like to formally introduce my new sister-in-law.
She was formerly my next door neighbor.

former: earlier in a list or group of two
latter: last in a list or group of two
Here are Mary and Paul. The former is my sister; the latter, my brother.

forth: forward
fourth: number four in order
Go forth and multiply. Everyone except the fourth guy from the end—the little ugly guy.

freeze: chill to a solid
frieze: a decorated band (often on a building)
The Greek ruins are interesting, dear—especially the frieze on that one—but I want to go back to the hotel. I'm freezing.

gait: manner of walking

gate: opening in wall or fence

That horse has such an uneven gait, I was sore and tired by the time we got to the gate.

gild: (v) cover with gold

gilt: (n) gold, or something that looks like gold, covering a surface

guilt: lack of innocence

Today we will learn how to gild picture frames.

Where is the bottle of gilt?

You may deny your guilt, but I see gold under your fingernails.

good: an adjective

well: an adverb

It is a good thing you did well on the test.

hangar: where a plane is stored

hanger: something used to hang

The pilot's uniform is on a hanger in the hangar.

hear: listen

here: this place

Now hear this: if you want ice cream, you'd better come here.

hoard: (n) a hidden supply; (v) to gather and store
horde: a crowd
> *Hordes of people started to hoard milk and bread after they heard about the hurricane.*

holey: full of holes
holy: sacred
wholly: entirely
> *I took a holey sack of mint to Sunday school when I was six.*
> *It turned out I was supposed to take the holy sacrament.*
> *I was wholly embarrassed.*

hours: periods of sixty minutes
ours: belonging to us
> *The hours we spent talking at the lake last night will be ours forever, even if you do marry Mabel.*

human: relating to people
humane: compassionate
> *Wouldn't it be nice if all humans were humane?*

idle: useless; inactive
idol: object of devotion
> *All this idle chatter about the matinee idol is wasting our time.*

immoral: not ethical

immortal: living forever

Jim's immoral behavior made the priest fear for the boy's immortal soul

immunity: protection from

impunity: without penalty

The ambassador has diplomatic immunity, and he apparently feels he can violate traffic rules with impunity.

impossible: not possible according to its nature

impracticable: not possible according to the circumstance

improbable: unlikely

It is impossible to go ice fishing in a skating rink.

It is impracticable to go ice fishing before the ice is very thick.

It is improbable I will ever go ice fishing.

impassable: incapable of being passed

impassible: incapable of feeling

The Donner party was stranded when the path became impassable.

After the horrors they suffered, many of them were impassible—a common defense mechanism.

imply: suggest a meaning (person speaking implies)

infer: draw a conclusion (person hearing infers)

I implied you had too much work; you inferred I meant you were lazy.

incredible: unbelievable

incredulous: unbelieving

I find it incredible that you are still incredulous after seeing the proof with your own eyes.

indiscreet: lacking judgment

indiscrete: not separated into parts

Spreading rumors about your boss was indiscreet.

Someone's personality is an indiscrete combination of their experiences, interests and abilities.

inequity: injustice

iniquity: wickedness

The inequity of the situation makes me furious.

His iniquity is going unpunished while his victims continue to suffer.

infect: contaminate

infest: spread or swarm

You'd better wash that cut, or it might get infected.

Crime infested this neighborhood after the unemployment rate soared.

ingenious: clever
ingenuous: innocent

Acting as ingenuous as a young girl was an ingenious and devious trick to get his attention.

it's: contraction of it is
its: third-person singular possessive pronoun

It's the third time the cat has caught its tail in the screen door.

knead: push and pull with the hands
kneed: struck with the knee
need: want

My mother taught me how to knead bread. She also told me how she kneed a man who tried to attack her in the park.

She demonstrates so many sides of being a woman, I don't think I need another role model.

ladder: structure for climbing up or down
later: more recent in time
latter: last in a group of things

> *My mother reminded me to pick up a ladder at the hardware store while I was out.*
> *I told my mother and father I would bring home dinner later.*
> *The latter asked me to bring Chinese food because Mom never cooks it.*

lay: to put down; past tense of lie
lie: to rest in horizontal position
> *After you lay the newspaper on the desk, it will lie there until someone moves it.*

lead (short *e* sound): heavy metal
lead (long *e* sound): guide or direct
led: past tense of lead (guide)
> *Lead can protect Superman from kryptonite. Watch the bads guys lead Jimmy and Lois into a trap.*
> *A little boy in the front row of the theater led the chorus of "Don't go, Jimmy" and "Look out, Lois."*

lean: low in fat; incline
lien: charge on property to satisfy a debt
> *The tall, lean man on the right (leaning against the wall) is from the finance company.*
> *He just filed a lien on your house, because you didn't pay for the aluminum siding.*

learn: gain knowledge

teach: instruct

We teach what we know and can only hope you will learn it.

leave: go away

let: allow

Let the skunk finish eating the cat's food, and maybe it will leave quietly.

legislator: law maker

legislature: hall of government

The legislature is full of legislators and lobbyists.

lends: makes a loan

lens: piece of curved, transparent material

If the bank lends us money, we'll start production of a new lens for the observatory.

lessen: make less

lesson: something learned

Learning a lesson from your error lessens the odds of repeating the mistake.

lesser: of less size, quantity, etc.

lessor: one who leases property

The landlord couldn't decide on the lesser of two evils: allowing the lessors to keep pets or having to evict them.

let's: contraction of *let us*
lets: allows
> *Let's go to Paul's house; his wife lets us smoke inside.*

levee: embankment to prevent flooding
levy: an assessment
> *The town council passed a levy on new businesses to pay for the levee on the river.*

liable: responsible
libel: unfavorable statement
> *I'll see that you are held legally liable for the libel you are spreading about me.*

lie: untruth; recline
lye: caustic chemical
> *It is no lie that lye will eat right through the crud that lies in the sink trap.*

loath: reluctant
loathe: detest
> *I am loath to be alone with that man.*
> *I loathe everything he stands for.*

loose: not tight
lose: misplace
> *That bracelet is so loose, you may lose it.*

luxuriant: abundant
luxurious: marked by luxury

She is attractive to men because of her luxuriant hair and luxurious clothes.

magnate: business person of rank or power
magnet: body that attracts iron
Because power is an aphrodisiac, the oil magnate attracts women like a magnet.

manner: style
manor: mansion
She changed every manner of her life after she moved into the manor.

many: a large number (things you can count)
much: a large amount (things you cannot count)
He made too much of a fuss over how many pairs of shoes I bought.

marry: to wed
merry: happy
The merry couple will marry on Sunday.

marshal: law enforcement or government official
martial: related to the military
I know the governor can declare martial law, but I don't really believe the fire marshal can.

marital: related to marriage
martial: related to the military

> *Martial affairs often include brass bands, while extramarital affairs usually involve soft music.*

material: relating to matter

materiel: equipment or supplies

> *What you can see and touch is referred to as the material world.*
> *A worker who orders supplies could be called a materiel specialist.*

may: used with a present tense main verb

might: used with a past tense main verb

> *The office manager says I may have the afternoon off.*
> *Yesterday she said Paul might take this afternoon off.*

miner: worker in a mine

minor: young person or inconsequential thing

> *Since child labor laws were passed, employing a minor as a miner is not a minor offense.*

moat: a trench, usually filled with water, around a castle

mote: a speck

> *The guard was blinded by the mote in his eye and fell into the moat.*

moral: ethical

morale: sense of well being
Employee morale will suffer if the boss keeps trying to impose his moral code on us.

morality: virtue
mortality: being subject to death
People sometimes reexamine their morality during a mid-life crisis.
Becoming aware of your own mortality can lead to many changes.

morning: time before noon
mourning: period of grief
We will be mourning his death at the funeral tomorrow morning.

motif: theme
motive: reason for doing something
You can't help wondering what her motive was for using a prison motif for the wedding shower.

muscle: part of the body, strength
mussel: ocean shellfish
It takes some muscle to open a mussel shell.

odious: distasteful
odorous: having odor
Hauling odorous garbage is an odious task no one wants to do.

official: authorized

officious: meddlesome
> *My mother-in-law is so officious, we've declared her an official pain in the rear.*

omnipotent: all-powerful
omniscient: all-knowing
> *Because the supervisor has the power to hire and fire, he thinks he is omnipotent. My teenaged daughter thinks she is omniscient—she has all the answers.*

ordinance: rule
ordnance: guns
> *There is an ordinance forbidding civilians to own that kind of ordnance.*

organism: living being
orgasm: sexual climax
> *Not all organisms experience orgasms.*

pail: bucket
pale: lacking color
> *You better put down that heavy pail before you faint. You look pale.*

pain: discomfort
pane: piece of something (often glass)
> *Of course I'm in pain.*
> *I dropped a pane of glass on my bare foot.*

pair: group of two

pare: to peel
pear: fruit

I'm going to pare a pair of pears; would you like one?

palate: roof of the mouth; sense of taste
palette: surface for mixing paints; set of colors
pallet: portable platform

Chocolate always satisfies my palate.
Computer drawing programs often have more than one palette to chose from.
You'll need to use a forklift to move that pallet.

palpate: examine by touch
palpitate: throb

The doctor palpated my stomach.
When he hit the painful spot, my heart palpitated and I gasped.

parameter: characteristic element
perimeter: boundary of flat surface

One of the parameters of the geometry problem is the perimeter of the circle.

parlay: transform to greater value
parley: confer with

I'm going to parley with my friend at the track, and see if I can't parlay a few small bets into some big money.

passed: past tense of pass

past: time gone by

> *The man we just passed—no, don't look—*
> *is a past boyfriend of mine.*

peace: calm, without strife

piece: portion

> *Let's enjoy the peace and quiet with a piece*
> *of cake and a cup of tea.*

peal: ringing of bells; loud sound

peel: fruit or vegetable skin

> *Did you hear the peals of laughter when*
> *the clown slipped on the banana peel?*

pedal: a foot lever; to use a foot lever

peddle: sell

petal: flower part

> *Don't try to peddle your petals here. I'll*
> *pedal my bike to the fields and pick my*
> *own flowers.*

pediatric: related to medical treatment of children

podiatric: related to medical treatment of the foot

> *After describing my podiatric problem, fallen*
> *arches, to the doctor I met at your party,*
> *I was embarrassed to find out he was a*
> *pediatric specialist.*

peer: an equal

pier: landing place for ships
The gentleman found no peers among the longshoremen on the pier.

penal: related to prison
penile: related to the penis
Some people believe our penal system needs reform.
The wonder drug correcting penile disfunction will make millions of dollars.

persecute: cause suffering
prosecute: bring legal action against
Civilized people don't persecute each other.
Society must prosecute wrongdoers, or laws will lose their meanings.

personal: individual
personnel: group of people, usually employees
The office personnel made personal decisions about contributing to the boss's birthday present.

perspective: point of view
prospective: likely
From my perspective, she looks like a prospective employee.

physic: medicinal preparation
physique: form of a person's body

psychic: (adj) sensitive to supernatural forces; (n) a person who is sensitive to supernatural forces

The psychic suggested my brother buy a physic to improve his physique.

picture: image of something

pitcher: container for liquids; baseball player

Did you get a picture of the Dodger's pitcher after his teammates poured the pitcher of water over him?

pillow: a cushion

pillar: a column; a support

The emperor is the fat guy lying on a pillow next to the last pillar on the left.

plain: not fancy; flat land

plane: airplane; tool for smoothing wood; a level of existence; a level surface

It's a plain fact that flying a plane over the plains takes me to a higher plane of consciousness.

plaintiff: one who files a law suit

plaintive: melancholy

After the judge ruled for the defendant, the plaintiff let out a plaintive cry and collapsed to the floor.

poor: poverty-stricken or pitiful

pore: a small opening; to read intently

pour: to flow in a stream

You poor thing. The sweat is pouring out of your pores as you pore over that book.

portent: omen

potent: powerful

In Boston, a robin is a portent of spring. After a long winter, that robin is a potent symbol of upcoming relief.

practical: useful

practicable: possible

Making your own soap is practicable, but not very practical.

pray: address God or beg a person

prey: (n) hunted animal or helpless person; (v) to hunt or exploit

I suppose I should pray for people who prey on young children.

precede: go before

proceed: continue

procedure: method of doing

A planning meeting probably should precede the new product announcement.
Are you going to proceed with the original schedule?

*I am interested in seeing how your proce-
dure works.*

precedence: preference
precedents: things that may set an example for
future actions
*Requests from the front office take prece-
dence over regularly scheduled tasks.*
*If we make exceptions for sales and mar-
keting, we could be setting precedents that
will come back to haunt us.*

premise: something taken for granted
premises: a building and its surrounding grounds
*Your premise that you could wander the
premises unescorted was wrong.*

prescribe: lay down a rule of action
proscribe: forbid
The doctor prescribed complete bed rest.
He proscribed any travelling.

presence: the act of being present
presents: gifts
*The only presents I want for my birthday
are your presence and a new car.*

presumptive: thought to be truth without proof
presumptuous: taking liberties
*You endanger your presumptive innocence
with that attitude.*

Asking the prosecutor where he buys his ties and other presumptuous behavior doesn't help your case.

preview: see beforehand
purview: range of authority
It is within his purview as school principal to preview the senior class play.

primer: (pronounced with a long *i* sound) first coat of paint or color
primer: (pronounced with a short *i* sound) small introductory book
primmer: more prudish
I told him I thought using red paint as primer for the bathroom walls was a bad idea.
The primer on painting said to use light colors.
If my aunt were any primmer, she wouldn't even have a bathroom.

principal: (adj) the most important; (n) head person; (n) money drawing interest
principle: a law or rule
"The principal reason I'm here isn't to determine who is wrong. It is the principle of the matter," said the high school principal.

It may help to remember *principle* is only a noun, while *principal* can be a noun or adjective.

profit: to gain

prophet: one who sees the future

Genuine prophets don't charge money; only the phony psychics try to profit from your need to know what's coming up.

prone: lying face down

supine: lying face up

You say the body was prone with a knife sticking out of the chest.

I think you mean the body was supine.

propose: offer a plan

purpose: intention

I propose we have a meeting to discuss the purpose of the organization.

qualify: restrict

quantify: measure quantity

I can't quantify my love for you; it is immeasurable and unqualified.

quarts: measurement equaling two pints

quartz: a crystalline mineral

I need three quarts of oil.

I found my grandfather's old quartz-crystal radio in the attic.

quiet: not loud

quit: stop

quite: completely

Be quiet or the guard will hear us.
Quit goofing around.
Our lawyer wasn't quite good enough, I'm sorry to say.

rack: framework objects are placed on
wrack: ruin or destroy
I've wracked my brain, but I can't figure out why the new line of styrofoam racks isn't selling.

rain: water drops that fall from the sky
rein: (v) restrain; (n) a strap to control an animal
reign: to rule; the time when a ruler reigns
I don't think the rain is ever going to stop.
You had better rein in your imagination, before it gets you into trouble.
The reign of Louis XIV of France did not end well.

raise: lift up
raze: tear down
rays: streams of particles or energy travelling in a straight line
We want to raise the property values downtown.
We're going to raze a couple of the abandoned warehouses.

> *Clearing out that area offers some faint rays of hope.*

raise: lift up (takes an object)

rise: move upward (doesn't take an object)

> *Keeping life in perspective may help raise your spirits.*
>
> *No matter how bad things seem, the sun will probably rise tomorrow.*

rapped: knocked

rapt: engrossed (adjective)

wrapped: engrossed (verb)

> *I was so wrapped up in the book, he had rapped several times before he interrupted my rapt attention to Rhett and Scarlett.*

rational: logical

rationale: underlying reason

> *Being afraid of the dark may not be rational, but it's my rationale for sleeping with the lights on.*

read: get meaning from, most often words

reed: tall grass

> *Sit still, and I will read you the story of the baby Moses in the reeds.*

real: actual

reel: revolving device with something wound on it

*My dad can do some real fishing now that
he has a new reel for his rod.*

rear: bring up a child
raise: grow a plant or bring an animal to maturity
You could tell he was reared by wolves.
He raises mushrooms under his bed.

remuneration: compensation
renumeration: NO SUCH WORD
*The landlord expects remuneration for the
property damage your last party caused.*

rest: all the other meanings (too many to list here)
wrest: pull away with violent movements
*After wresting the stick from me, the puppy
collapsed to rest awhile.*

retch: make an effort to vomit
wretch: unhappy or vile person
*I heard a horrible retching sound, then I
saw the poor wretch in the alley.*

reverend: worthy of respect: member of the clergy
reverent: worshipful
*His reverent tone shows his respectful at-
titude toward his reverend father.*

review: critical evaluation; look over again
revue: theatrical production, usually loosely connected acts

After reviewing his notes, the newspaper critic gave the musical revue a bad review.

right: correct; not left; entitled power or privilege
rite: ceremony
wright: worker, usually combined with subject of the work
write: put down words, compose

Get enough right answers on the test, make your right turns and you will earn the right to drive a car.

Getting a driver's license is a rite of passage for most teenagers.

My brother is a playwright.

He writes embarrassing plays about our family.

ring: circular-shaped object
wring: to twist

Let's look for your missing ring.

Sitting here wringing your hands won't accomplish anything.

rot: to spoil
wrought: worked into shape

The new wrought iron patio furniture won't rot as the wooden table did.

rye: a grain
wry: cleverly humorous

I'll make you a ham on rye sandwich if you want one.

He is such a ham he makes wry comments more often than he should.

saccharin: artificial sweetener
saccharine: relating to sugar or overly sweet
   "Please pass the saccharin," she cooed in her saccharine voice.

scene: part of a play; locale; situation
seen: past participle of see
   I had never seen anything as disgraceful as that scene between my husband and his father.

sea: ocean
see: look at
   If you look over here, you can see the sea.

seam: a joining of two pieces
seem: give the impression of
   I can't seem to get this seam straight.

seasonable: suitable to the season
seasonal: relating to the season
   It is unseasonably warm for January.
   Snow skiing is a seasonal sport.

secretively: not open or outgoing
secretly: hidden

She is acting so secretively, I bet she's secretly shy.

sensual: indulgence of physical appetites as an end to itself
sensuous: gratification of the senses for aesthetic pleasure

Topless dancers are considered sensual, but a Rubens painting is called sensuous.

serge: durable twilled fabric
surge: to rise and fall

I watched his chest surge under his blue serge jacket.

sew: use needle and thread
sow: scatter seed
so: in a manner or way

My grandmother sews in the living room and sows in the garden.
She is always so busy she doesn't get bored.

shall: mandatory (in laws and regulations); expresses what seems inevitable
(You may have learned in school that the first person form of *will* should be *shall*. That just doesn't happen in common usage. I wouldn't argue with an English teacher about it, but I wouldn't use it in conversation, either.)
should: expresses an obligation or condition

would: expresses habit, condition or determination

> *City Council members shall live within the city limits.*
>
> *The valley shall flood, if the rain continues at this rate.*
>
> *I should finish this report tonight.*
>
> *If I should finish the report early enough, we could go to a movie.*
>
> *I would always put off unpleasant jobs until the last minute.*
>
> *I would have done it sooner, if it weren't so hard.*
>
> *I would like to go to the movies tonight.*

shear: (n) scissors; (v) cut

sheer: very thin; unmixed; steep

> *We're going to shear sheep in the morning.*
>
> *It took sheer gall to wear that sheer blouse to the office.*
>
> *Be careful, it's a sheer drop from here to the river.*

simulate: imitate

stimulate: excite to activity or growth

> *A rise in diamond prices stimulated the simulated gem industry.*

sleight: deceitful craftiness

slight: slim; meager

Watch out for that slightly built man in the corner. He is a sleight of hand artist and will take your money.

sniffle: sniff repeatedly
snivel: whine
Please blow your nose and stop sniffling.
I don't like snivelling kids.

soar: rise dramatically
sore: painful, a wound
The stock's soaring price is a sore point with my dad—he sold last week.

sole: bottom of the foot or shoe; flatfish; solitary
soul: spiritual aspect of being; relating to Black culture
The sole reason I'm eating fried sole is because I cannot afford steak after getting my boots resoled.
Soul music from Harlem feeds my soul.

solid: serious in character
stolid: unemotional
He's such a solid citizen, he'd never break the law.
He's such a stolid individual, you'll never see him laugh.

somewhere: unnamed place; approximately

somewheres: NOT A PREFERRED WORD
He's got to be somewhere around here.

stalactite: icicle-like, mineral growth from the ceiling of caves
stalagmite: icicle-like, mineral growth from the floor of caves
I remember stalacTites come from the Top and stalagMites come from the bottoM. You might want to remember stalaCtites come from the Ceiling and stalaGmites come from the Ground.

stationary: not moving
stationery: paper for writing letters
If my life-style were stationary, I wouldn't need so much stationery to write letters to distant friends.

statue: three-dimensional model of a person, animal, etc.
stature: height or status
statute: law
Vandals attacked Washington's statue in the park last night.
Don't they have any respect for a man of his stature?
We need to toughen the statutes against graffiti.

stay: remain

stop: cease activity

> *Stop screaming! Now stay quiet.*

suppose: think something is probable

supposed: required

> *I suppose I could lend you some money.*
> *You were supposed to have repaid my last*
> *loan by now, though.*

suspect: (v) to imagine something is true, usually without complete proof; (n) someone suspected, especially of a crime

suspicion: a noun only

> *I suspect we'll pick up a suspect today.*
> *I have a suspicion that you know more*
> *about that robbery than you are telling us.*

systematic: thorough, methodical

systemic: common to a system

> *The botanist performed a systematic study*
> *of all the plants in our area.*
> *That systemic pesticide will end up in the*
> *fruit as well as on the leaves.*

tail: the rear end

tale: a story

> *Don't close the tailgate of the truck on the*
> *dog's tail!*
> *My Uncle Fred used to tell the greatest*

tales of his adventures in the South Pacific.

team: a group working together
teem: filled to overflowing
The stadium teemed with fans of the winning football team.

tenant: a person who rents
tenet: a principle or belief
Our tenant is months behind in the rent.
Paying rent is a basic tenet of rental economics.

tern: a kind of sea gull
turn: all the other dozens of meanings, except sea gull!
Turn around—see the tern on the pier?

than: a conjunction used in comparisons
then: an adverb relating to time
Is your temperature higher than 103?
If it is, then it is time to call the doctor.

that: pronoun introducing essential information
which: pronoun introducing unessential information
I bought the car that had been kept in a garage.
The sentence implies I had a choice between a car kept in a garage and one parked outside.

I bought the car, which had been kept in a garage.

This time I'm just telling you something extra about the car. Its being stored in a garage apparently didn't influence me.

their: third-person plural possessive
there: that place
they're: contraction of they are
  They're taking their cat to the vet over there.

theirs: third-person plural pronoun
there's: contraction of there is
  There's no reason to take theirs to a different vet.

thorough: complete; careful with detail
through: from one end or side to the other
threw: past tense of throw
  I did a thorough search of the refrigerator. Then, I looked through the freezer.
  Everything was better after I threw away the moldy oranges.

throes: spasm; painful struggle
throws: casts; tosses
  It was a bad idea to visit my brother while he was in the throes of a divorce.
  He sits and throws darts at her picture.

throne: place of honor, usually for king or queen
thrown: past tense of throw
> *The throne sits empty.*
> *The rebels have thrown out the rulers.*

tic: twitch or spasm
tick: bloodsucking bug
> *He's so worried about Lyme disease since*
> *he found that tick, he has a nervous tic.*

tide: rising and falling of ocean surface
tied: formed a knot or bow
> *I hope you tied the boat tightly, so it won't*
> *float away with the tide.*

to: indicates movement toward
too: also
two: number between one and three
> *Are you going to the movies?*
> *I want to come, too.*
> *The two of us could have lots of fun.*

toad: frog-like animal
toed: relating to toes
towed: pulled
> *They towed a four-foot long, seven-toed toad*
> *out of the toxic dump.*

tort: act that could lead to legal civil action
torte: kind of cake

I asked my attorney if food poisoning from a chocolate torte was a tort.

tortuous: winding
torturous: cruelly painful
Walking up and down the tortuous steps of the ruins all day was torturous.

try and: WRONG
try to: this is the proper form
Try to remember not to use try and.

turbid: muddy; foul
turgid: pompous
The turbid water made rescue difficult.
His turgid speech makes us laugh.

undo: reverse; destroy
undue: exceeding what is proper
A police officer's use of undue force would undo the public trust we worked so hard to build.

unequivocally: without reservation
unequivocably: NO SUCH WORD
The City Council unequivocally passed the resolution praising the firefighter's bravery.

urban: relating to a city
urbane: suave

Many urban kids have never seen a cow.
Cary Grant played urbane characters.

use: carry out a purpose
utilize: suggests new or profitable use of something

If you use your imagination, I bet you could find a way to utilize all that scrap paper.

People have decided *use* is too plain, and they use *utilize* when *use* is really what they mean.

vain: conceited; unsuccessful
vane: movable device showing wind direction
vein: blood vessel or suggesting a vein; style

His vain attempts at humor never make us laugh, but he is so vain, he thinks he's funny.

She bought a weather vane shaped like a flying pig.

Jokes of that vein don't go down around here.

valance: a short drapery
valence: property of a chemical element

She is the only one who thought the purple valance over the living room window was attractive.

I got a B on my chemistry test because I couldn't remember the valence of iron.

variance: difference

variants: two or more things that differ slightly

We have a variance in monthly profits.

Flammable and inflammable are variants of the same word.

vary: partial change

very: truly

His attitude can vary from moment to moment, and I find that very disturbing.

veracious: truthful

voracious: insatiable

Though it is tempting to lie, I try to be veracious.

My teenage son's appetite is voracious.

vertex: the point farthest from the base of a figure

vortex: fluid whirling in circular motion

The whirlpool vortex was at the vertex of the mountain.

vice: moral fault

vise: tool for holding work

Chocolate is my only vice.

After you glue the wood, put it into the vise while it dries.

visible: capable of being seen

visual: relating to vision

In good visual effects, the tricks are not visible.

waist: part of the body above hips
waste: (v) squander; (n) scrap; (n) barren land
I'm throwing away these pants, because the waist doesn't fit me now.
I always clean my plate, because I can't stand to waste anything.

wait: linger
weight: measure of heaviness
I'll wait for an hour, but then I'm going without you.
He has lost so much weight, you won't recognize him.

wafer: thin cookie or cracker
waiver: giving up a requirement
waver: to hesitate
Is it blasphemy to say the wafer tasted stale?
He got a waiver for his bad eye sight.
He never wavered in his desire to become a policeman.

waive: voluntarily give up
wave: (v) salute; (v) flutter; (n) an ocean swell
He waived his right to a jury trial.

We waved at the ship as it headed out over the waves, the American flag waving on deck.

wale: even rib in fabric
wail: prolonged cry or sound
whale: large sea mammal
I'll have three yards of that wide-wale corduroy, please.
Listen to the wail of the wind.
All the folks from the office are going whale-watching tomorrow.

walk: move on foot
wok: cooking pan with steep sides
It's too far to walk to the store.
Madeline stir-fried chicken in the wok.

ware: manufactured articles, goods
wear: put on as clothing
where: what place
I gave my daughter earthenware dishes as a wedding present.
I've never seen her wear the vest I gave her for Christmas.
I don't know where my mother finds the ugly gifts she gives.

way: method or path
weigh: measure heaviness; evaluate

whey: watery part of milk that remains when cheese is made

That is no way to weigh whey.

weak: not strong
week: seven days

My hamster looks weak.
I suppose he does: you haven't fed him since last week.

weather: state of the atmosphere—temperature, humidity, wind, etc.
whether: alternate conditions

We are going to the beach whether the weather is nice or not.

who's: contraction of who is
whose: possessive of who

Whose elephant is in my backyard?
Who's going to help me clean up after the elephant?

will: used with a present tense main verb
would: used with a past tense main verb

He says he will help me today.
He told me on Thursday he would help me today.

yoke: wooden frame to join two work animals; piece at top of shirt

yolk: the yellow part of an egg
> *How did you get egg yolk on the yoke of your good blouse?*

yore: long ago
your: possessive of you
you're: contraction of you are
> *You're showing your age when you tell so many stories about days of yore.*

My editor has a few more to add. Break out the dictionary and see if you can determine how these pairs of words differ from each other:

away and *aweigh*

every day and *everyday*

hardly and *heartily*

moot and *mute*

sooth and *soothe*

want and *wont*

Letter Writing

Letter writing used to be far more common than it is today. Romances and business deals were started and sometimes completed on paper. The telephone call increasingly replaced the letter over the past fifty years. Computer e-mail just may bring back the letter. People are rediscovering the convenience of writing. The best parts of letter writing are you can do it on your schedule and you can take the time to say exactly what you want to. It is often difficult to connect with the person you want to speak with, and telephone conversations have a way of wandering off the subject.

Business letters

A business letter has six parts: heading, inside address, salutation, body, closing and signature.

The heading is the sender's address and the date the letter is written. If you have letterhead stationery, you only need the date in the heading. The date should be written with unabbreviated words. Double space after the last line of the heading.

November 15, 1998
not *Nov. 15, 1998*
not *11/15/98*

The inside address is the name, company name and address of the person receiving the letter. If you are writing to a company and do not know a person's name, use a title or department name. Your letter may get more attention, though, if you call the company to get a name to address the letter to.

Customer Service
Liberty Insurance, Inc.
435 Main Street
Hartford CT 03456

Do not abbreviate anything but the state name, unless the company uses abbreviations in its name. Notice we don't use a comma between the city and state abbreviation. This is the style the U.S. Postal Service prefers. The envelope should be addressed the same way. Double space again after the inside address.

The salutation starts with *Dear*. What follows next depends on how well you know the person you are writing to. Use *Mr.* or *Ms. Lastname:* unless you personally know the recipient. Notice there is no first name. When speaking, you wouldn't call someone Mr. John Smith. You'd say, Mr. Smith. The colon is becoming optional, but when you write to a stranger you can't go wrong with the more formal style. If you know the person you are writing to well enough to use the first name, use a comma, not a colon. Double space after the salutation.

Dear Mr. Jones:
or *Dear Jim,*

The body of the letter may be written with indented paragraphs or blocks of text with extra space between paragraphs. There are variations, but these are the two most popular. You may use either and be correct. Double space after the body of the letter.

The closing is your farewell. Capitalize only the first word and end with a comma. Here are some commonly-used closings. Use a closing that fits with the letter's message and recipient. You probably don't want to close a letter threatening a law suit with *Cordially yours. Respectfully yours* is too formal for a letter to a business acquaintance.

Yours truly,
Yours very truly,
Very truly yours,
Sincerely,

Yours sincerely,
Sincerely yours,
Respectfully,
Yours respectfully,
Respectfully yours,
Cordially,
Yours cordially,
Cordially yours,

The letter's signature includes your typewritten or hand-printed name as well as your written signature. Triple space after the closing before typing or printing your name. You may add your title after or under your typed name, if it is appropriate. Sign your name between the closing and your typed name.

James Colburn, Director
Public Relations

Mariel Brown, Vice-president

Heading
xxxx XXXXX XXXXX
XXXXXX XX xxxxx
Date

Inside address
xxxx XXXXX XXXXX
XXXXXX XX xxxxx

Salutation:

Every line is flush left. XXX XXXXX XX
XXXXX XXXX XX XXX XXXXX XXX XXXX
XXX XXXXX XX XXXXX XXXX XX XXX
XXXXX XXX XXXX XXX XXXXX XX
XXXXX XXXX XX XXX XXXXX XXX XXXX

XXX XXXXX XX XXXXX XXXX XX XXX
XXXXX XXX XXXX XXX XXXXX XX
XXXXX XXXX XX XXX XXXXX XXX XXXX

XXX XXXXX XX XXXXX XXXX XX XXX
XXXXX XXX XXXX XXX XXXXX XX XXX

Closing,

Name
Title

Heading
xxxx XXXXX XXXXX
XXXXXX XX xxxxx
Date

Inside address
xxxx XXXXX XXXXX
XXXXXX XX xxxxx

Salutation:

Each paragraph is indented. XXX
XXXXX XX XXX XX XXXX XX XXX
XXXXX XXX XXXX XXX XXXXX XX
XXXXX XXXX XX XXX XXXXX XXX XXXX
XXX XXXXX XX XXXXX XXXX XX XXX
XXXXX

XXX XXXXX XX XXXXX XXXX XX
XXX XXXXX XXX XXXX XXX XXXXX XX
XXXXX XXXX XX XXX XXXXX XXX XXXX
XXX XXXXX XX XXXXX XXXX XX
XXX XXXXX XXX XXXX XXX XXXXX XX
XXX

Closing,

Name
Title

These letter forms are adapted from *Write Perfect Letters for Any Occasion* by R. Emil Neuman and used with permission of United Research Publishers.

Business letter mechanics

Business letters should be written on letterhead or plain, neutral-colored, 8-1/2 by 11 inch paper. Margins should be no less than an inch on each side, top and bottom. If the letter is short, start the heading low on the page. You want the letter to be roughly centered on the page. If the letter is really short, you can make the right and left margins wider (remember that trick from term papers?).

Letters should be folded into thirds, bottom third folded up first. It should go into the business-sized envelope with the open end up and facing the flap.

The rule used to be that envelopes must be type-written. In the age of computers and junk mail, some people see a hand-addressed envelope as a welcome, personal touch. Use your judgment.

Business letter body

Letter writing doesn't have to be difficult. Most people only expect understandable sentences. If you have a serious writer's block when it comes to letter writing, start with notes to yourself about what you want to say. Jot down the main points you want to make. Use just a word or phrase for each point. Then turn those words or phrases into sentences. Arrange the sentences in logical order. You now have the skeleton of your letter.

If you are writing to complain about shoddy merchandise or bad service, a first draft is very important. Few of us think clearly when we are upset. What you write while you are upset serves well as a first draft, but rewrite it after you have cooled off. You'll probably be able to reorganize the letter so its meaning is clearer. Don't mail a letter you write while you are angry. The letter you mail should sound reasonable and unemotional. Most companies want to hear from unsatisfied customers, as final quality control, but a written tirade full of fury is bound to irritate the reader.

Remember to include all the necessary information in your letter. Identify yourself. Indicate how the reader can contact you. Explain why you are writing. Indicate what you want the reader to do for you. Include account numbers so the recipient can find you in the company records, if necessary. If the letter is a follow-up to a phone call, list the main points of the conversation to refresh the recipient's mind.

Business letters call for a more formal style than social letters, but don't try to be too formal. Write with words you use when you speak. If you try to use words that are not in your normal vocabulary, there is a real danger you will misuse them. That doesn't impress anyone. Another common fault that doesn't impress people is using what we call inflated words.

Inflated words

We are coming out of a period of word inflation. For many years people have used fifty-cent words or phrases, instead of common words, to try to sound more educated or important than they really are. Government and educational institution employees have been the worst offenders. Recently the federal government decided to go back to plain language. There are now federal employees translating gobbledygook into English people can actually understand.

Here are some examples of words and phrases you may see in business correspondence and the preferred alternatives:

Inflated	Better
endeavor	try
feasible	possible
equitable	fair
ascertain	discover

Inflated	**Better**
initiate	begin
consummate	complete
concur	agree
procure	get
verification	proof
reiterate	repeat
subsequently	after
tardy	late
for the purpose of	for
subsequent to	after
in the event that	if
reduce to a minimum	minimize
despite the fact that	though
sells at a price of	sells for
at a later date	later
at the present time	now
due to the fact that	since
in order to	to
inasmuch as	since
in the event that	if

Inflated	**Better**
in the normal course	normally
in the very near future	soon
in view of the fact	because
of the order of magnitude	about
prior to	before
pursuant to our agreement	as we agreed
will you be kind enough to	please
enclosed please find	I've enclosed
at an early date	soon
at all times	always
until such time as	until
in the course of	during
in compliance with your request	as requested
costs the sum of	costs
we regret to advise	we are sorry
keep in mind the fact that	remember that

Inflated	**Better**
at such time as you are in a position	when you can
being sold for a price of	sells for

Social letters

A social letter can be more casual than a business letter, but it should still be correct and have some style. In the past the rule was that social letters should be handwritten. Typed social letters are more acceptable today with a couple exceptions.

If you should get a formal invitation, say from the White House, you really need to hand write your response.

Letters of sympathy or condolence also should be handwritten. They need that personal touch to show warmth and concern. (Because they are probably the hardest letters to write, we will talk more about them later in the chapter.)

You do not need a heading or an inside address in a social letter. The salutation ends with a comma instead of a colon. The closing is more informal than a business letter closing. Your handwritten name is enough; you don't need to type or print your name and title under it.

Social letter mechanics

A social letter may be written on almost any kind of paper. You are freer to express your personality with social stationery. Matching paper and envelopes have an elegance we seldom see these days, but a friend or family member will probably be thrilled to get a cheery letter from you even on notebook paper.

Sympathy and condolence letters are the exception again.

Letters should be folded into thirds, bottom third folded up first. It should go into the envelope with the open end up and facing the flap.

Social letter body

There aren't many rules for social letters. We will address some for specific types of letters, but generally a social letter should reflect your personal style and relationship with the reader. You will probably write differently to your maiden aunt in Des Moines than you do to your childhood pal.

Think of yourself sitting with a cup of coffee and chatting with your relative or friend. What would you tell them about your life and family?

Letters of sympathy or condolence

Sympathy letters don't have to be difficult to write, though most people worry about them. A hand-written note on plain white paper is more appropriate than a purchased card. If you must buy a card, do add a written note.

A letter of condolence is not supposed to make the reader feel good about the bereavement. You write such a letter to express your sympathy. You can do that in only three or four sentences. In fact, shorter is better. Don't add news about your life or discuss the illness or accident that caused the death. Even if the deceased suffered through a long illness, it is considered improper to speak of death as a relief.

Here is an example of a perfectly fine letter of condolence:

Dear Diane,

Words cannot express my sorrow over your mother's death. She was loved and respected by all fortunate enough to have known her. She will be missed. John and I send our deepest sympathy.

Sincerely,
Carol

E-mail

E-mail is often full of sentence fragments, abbre- viations and phonetic spellings. Some people think that lack of structure is part of e-mail's appeal. Others think it signals the end of civilization as we know it.

Because electronic mail is so dynamic—a single click of the mouse can send it half way around the world faster than a heartbeat—it has an energy that resists rigid structure. Because it is so easy to send e-mail—we go back to that single click— people send short, frequent messages.

Folks who haven't written a letter since they went away to summer camp in fifth grade find them- selves corresponding regularly with old and new friends.

E-mail etiquette

While this new phenomenon is very casual, it does have its own rules.

TYPING IN ALL CAPS is the e-mail equivalent to shouting. Most people don't like it.

A descriptive phrase in the subject line is impor- tant because some people get hundreds of mes- sages a day and delete messages without reading them if the subject line doesn't get their attention.

Even though most folks don't seem to use salutations, I think they are a good idea. Frequently mail is sent to several people at once. Unless a message starts out with my name, or comes from my best friend, I assume I am just one of many recipients. A salutation gets my attention.

Another reason to use a salutation is that more than one person may use the same e-mail account. An entire family or office may be at the same e-mail address.

Closing with your name may not be necessary when you write to close friends: an initial or nickname might be enough for them.

People often don't use their last names when they correspond with people they only know through e-mail. One reason is for privacy. It is possible for someone other than the intended recipient to end up reading e-mail you send. It isn't common, but it is possible. You should remember that before you send out information you wouldn't want a stranger to have.

Employers sometimes monitor messages sent to their offices. If you are writing to someone's office or from your own, it is a good idea to avoid off-color and racist comments or jokes. It is not wise to share details of your love life, either. Your best friend's supervisor just might be reading all the mail that comes into the department.

Fun stuff

Here are some common abbreviations you may encounter in e-mail.

BTW   By the way

FAQ   Frequently asked questions

FWIW   For what it's worth

FYI   For your information

<g>   Grin

IMHO   In my humble opinion

IMNSHO   In my not so humble opinion

IMO   In my opinion

LOL   Laughing out loud

L8R   Later

OTOH   On the other hand

ROTFL   Rolling on the floor laughing

TIA   Thanks in advance

WYSIWYG   What you see is what you get

Writing Everything Else

We are going to look at what's called expository writing—writing designed to give information. Business reports and memos, magazine articles, non-fiction books and job descriptions all fall into this category. It is the kind of writing most of us do.

Whether you need to explain to a customer why a $4 million project won't be delivered on time or write a job description for the substitute receptionist, the process is the same.

Good writing breaks down into four tasks:

> have something to say
>
> concentrate on what you have to say
>
> build good sentences
>
> put those sentences together so they say what you want them to

When you can do those four things, you are a good writer.

Writing is less intimidating when you recognize those four tasks as separate things. When you are working on what you have to say, don't start worrying about your first paragraph. Concentrate on each task in its turn, and after you do each of them you will have a piece of writing you are proud to put your name on.

Have something to say

Before you start writing, think about the information you need to share with the reader. Don't worry about putting things in the right order. At this point, you just want to make sure you know what you want to say. You may find you need more information before you can start writing.

Quickly jot down the main points you want to make. Don't worry about putting them in the right order yet. Relax. Let your mind wander. When you think of something, write it down. Later you can decide if that point really belongs in what you are writing. Right now you want to think freely. No one else will see this, so don't worry about being logical, spelling correctly or being neat and tidy. You'll take care of those things later.

One technique professional writers use is to write the main point in the middle of an empty sheet of paper. Then they draw a circle around it. Ideas related to the main point are circled and connected to the main point with lines. Each point can lead to another idea.

The work you do before you actually start writing is probably the most important. It just might be the hardest, too. Most people have trouble allowing ideas to flow. Everyone can learn to do it with practice.

Concentrate on what you want to say

Now you start being logical. Look at all the ideas you wrote down and decide which ones you will use. If you did a good job of writing down ideas, you probably have many more than you actually need to use. That's fine. Odds are you came up with some ideas you would have missed if you hadn't done the free-thinking stage.

Think about what the reader needs to know to understand your main point. Most of the time readers don't need to know as much about the subject as you do. If you give them too much information, they may have trouble figuring out what you are trying to tell them. You want to give enough information to make your point and no more. Most of us have read two-page memos or letters full of facts and wondered why the writer told us all that.

On a fresh sheet of paper, put your ideas in logical order. Start with the first piece of information the reader needs to know. Look for the next thing on your page of ideas. After you have all the ideas you are going to use, look them over to see if there is anything you left out while you were thinking creatively. Put yourself in the reader's shoes to spot facts or issues you didn't write down.

Once you have all your ideas in place, you are ready to start writing. This is only the first draft, though, so don't concentrate on "pretty" writing. You'll do that in the next step.

Writing is difficult for some people because they try to do two or three things at once. They try to think creatively, structure the entire work logically and write good sentences. Those tasks each take concentration. Trying to do them simultaneously is as bad as trying to rub your stomach while you pat your head. You'll save energy and time if you do each of them separately.

Write as casually as you talk while you construct your report or memo. You are working on ideas now, not words. The task is to make sure each point follows logically from the one before as you build your ideas. This should go pretty fast.

Next you want to read through what you have written to make sure all the important ideas are there. Watch for unimportant things that crept in. It happens. Take them out.

Once you have read the entire piece and are satisfied you have included everything you need to say, you need to work on the individual paragraphs. Make sure each paragraph is only one main idea. If there is more than one thought in a paragraph, break it into two or more paragraphs. The paragraph should have what is called a topic sentence and information that expands the topic sentence. The topic sentence usually appears at the beginning or end of the paragraph. You either present the topic sentence and then offer details, or build up to the topic sentence. In some cases, you may build to the topic sentence with background information and then provide details after the topic sentence. That will put your topic sentence somewhere in the middle of the paragraph. Just make sure everything in the paragraph applies to the topic sentence. If you have something that doesn't belong to the topic sentence, you need another paragraph.

Build good sentences

Now that your ideas are in place, it is time to polish your sentences. You want each sentence to present information as clearly as possible. Good sentences are easy to understand. They follow the rules of grammar and use words appropriate for the reader. They vary in construction so reading them is interesting, but have a consistent style and tone. Even though an annual report may be more formal than an inter-office memo, it should be as easy to read.

Remember, communication is the purpose of writing. Writing should be clear—no ambiguity or confusion. Good grammar and sentence construction go a long way toward avoiding confusion. Grammar is covered earlier in the book, so there won't be much about it here.

Short sentences

Avoid long, complicated sentences. If your sentences tend to be very long, look at them carefully. You may be trying to say too much for one sentence to handle. You are less likely to have this problem when you follow the suggestions in the sections above. It can still happen, though, so watch for those cumbersome sentences and break them down into smaller ones. Lots of people have too much paper coming across their desks these days. If your writing is clean and crisp, your reader is more apt to react positively to you.

Common words

Each business or industry has its own specialized vocabulary called *jargon*. Be careful about using jargon. It is a convenient shorthand when talking to other people in your industry, but can be confusing to folks not familiar with it. The tricky thing is you may not even notice jargon, since it may be such a big part of your daily speech. If you write a lot for people outside your industry, it might be a good idea to make a list of words and phrases to avoid using with the outside world. You can check your final draft and substitute more appropriate language.

Use common words. You won't impress the right people with flowery language. Savvy, educated readers will recognize that you are trying to snow them. Less sophisticated readers may think you are smarter than they are, but they won't understand what you are trying to say. When you need to use a word you don't use in conversation, make sure it is the right word. Words with roughly the same meaning often have slightly different shades of meaning. *Climbing* and *clambering* are two examples. Check the dictionary if you have any doubts. You can refer to the list of commonly misused words included in this book, too.

The right words

You want to use accurate and precise words. Accurate means free of error; precise means sharply defined.

When you use inaccurate words, you lose the reader's confidence. If you use imprecise words, the reader may get the wrong idea of what you say or may have to spend time trying to figure out what you are saying.

Invoices must be submitted in triplicate to purchasing.

Make sure you mean invoices, not purchase orders.

Please attend the meeting next week.

This sentence is imprecise. What kind of meeting? When next week?

Please attend the sales meeting at 3:00 on Thursday, May 16.

This is a better sentence.

Picking the right verbs and nouns reduces your need for adverbs and adjectives. While there is nothing wrong with a colorful modifier, a strong verb or specific noun is better. Instead of announcing a casual, outdoor luncheon, call it a picnic.

The right words in the right order

Make sure you put together your sentences in a logical manner. Modifiers should be close to the words they modify. Objects should be close to their verbs or prepositions. Phrases and clauses should be close to what they refer to.

Probably the easiest way to understand this is to look at some examples. These sentences are funny because people didn't pay attention to what they wrote. See if you can rewrite the sentences so they are less amusing and more accurate.

My thanks to Richard Lederer for permission to use excerpts from *Anguished English* (Wyrick, Dell) and *More Anguished English* (Delacorte, Dell). Richard's amusing books are full of important, painless English lessons.

Mangling Modifiers

Please take time to look over the brochure that is enclosed with your family.

Farmhand Joe Mobbs hoists a cow injured while giving birth to its feet.

The police said Barth's 1981 Toyota traveled down the shoulder for almost 1,000 feet then hit a utility pole going about 45 miles per hour.

Here are some suggestions for handling obscene phone calls from New England Telephone Company.

The patient was referred to a psychiatrist with a severe emotional problem.

A 30-year-old St. Petersburg man was found murdered by his parents in his home late Saturday.

He rode his horse across Highway 12 and up and down the sidewalk in front of the saloon a good half hour before deputies arrived, shouting obscenities and being obnoxious.

Plunging 1,000 feet into the gorge, we saw Yosemite Falls.

Reference Wanted

Guilt, vengeance, and bitterness can be emotionally destructive to you and your children. You must get rid of them.

Jerry Remy then hit an RBI single off Haas's leg, which rolled into right field.

On the floor above him lived a redheaded instructor in physical education, whose muscular calves he admired when they nodded to each other by the mailbox.

People who use birth control methods that smoke a lot are in danger of having retarded children.

"He's the horse of a lifetime," said trainer Packy Lawrence. He'll retire after today's race and be shipped to Kentucky, where he'll begin a career at stud.

Extras

Because the garden party was partly in observance of the Year of the Disabled, the Queen and her family moved among the guests in wheelchairs and on crutches and aluminum walkers.

The bride was wearing an old lace gown that fell to the floor as she came down the aisle.

Have several very old dresses from grandmother in beautiful condition.

Wanted man to take care of cow that does not smoke or drink.

3-year-old teacher needed for pre-school.

Parallel construction

Parallel construction means writing similar things in the same manner. For example, don't mix participle phrases and gerund phrases in the same sentence. (You'll find participle and gerund phrases in the index!)

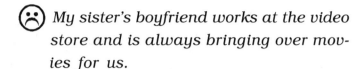 *My sister's boyfriend works at the video store and is always bringing over movies for us.*

My sister's boyfriend works at the video store and always brings over movies for us.

The lack of parallel construction also often shows up in lists.

Things to do:
   calling salesman
   need to assemble facts
   write report

See the difference when each point is constructed the same:

call salesman
assemble facts
write report

Every point has just a verb and an object for the verb, and each verb has the same form.

A little thing like parallel construction makes your writing appear more professional.

Proofreading

It is very difficult to proofread your own work. You know what you meant to say. Most of the time, you will see what you thought you said. The best idea is to ask someone else to look over what you write before you send it out. If that isn't practical, at least wait overnight before you try to proofread it. Reading aloud can help, too.

If you want to check your spelling, it is often helpful to read the work word for word—backwards. Start with the last word and work your way to the beginning. Reading backwards keeps you from getting caught up in the meaning of the words, forcing you to look at each word separately.

Last words

Writing doesn't have to be a horrible experience. Being able to do it well will bring you many rewards. Learning grammar and punctuation will help build your confidence. Writing and rewriting will sharpen your skills. The more you write, the better writer you become.

The biggest difference between good writers and poor ones is how much they care about getting their ideas cross to their readers. Good writers care enough to work at it.

Common Mistakes in English

Additional reading

The Elements of Style, William Strunk, Jr. and E.B. White. MacMillan Publishing Company

The Chicago Manual of Style. The University of Chicago Press

The Goof-Proofer, How to Avoid the 41 Most Embarrassing Errors in Your Speaking and Writing, Stephen J. Manhard. Collier Books

The Most Common Mistakes in English Usage, Thomas Elliott Berry. McGraw-Hill

Painless Perfect Grammar, Michael Strumpf and Auriel Douglas. Bandanna Books

The Well-Tempered Sentence, A Punctuation Handbook for the Innocent, the Eager, and the Doomed, Karen Elizabeth Gordon. Ticknor & Fields

What's in a Word, Mario Pei. Hawthorn Books, Inc.

Write Perfect Letters for Any Occasion, R. Emil Neuman. United Research Publishers

Common Mistakes in English

Index

Common Mistakes in English